Hilary Swank

by Dwayne Epstein

LUCENT BOOKS

An imprint of Thomson Gale, a part of The Thomson Corporation

THOMSON

GALE

Detroit • New York • San Francisco • San Diego • New Haven, Conn.
Waterville, Maine • London • Munich

YPB
Swank
Eps

THOMSON
GALE

LIBRARY OF CONGRESS CATALOGING-IN-PUBLICATION DATA

Epstein, Dwayne, 1960–
Hilary Swank / by Dwayne Epstein.
   p. cm. — (People in the news)
Includes bibliographical references and index.
Contents: Trailer park dreams—The art of persistence—Dreams do come true—The challenge of success—A force to be reckoned with—From this moment on.
ISBN 1-59018-856-X (hard cover : alk. paper)
1. Swank, Hilary—Juvenile literature. 2. Motion picture actors and actresses--United States—Biography—Juvenile literature. I. Title. II. Series: People in the news (San Diego, Calif.)
PN2287.S88E67 2006
791.4302'8092--dc22
[B]
                                                              2005031007

Printed in the United States of America

Contents

Fame and celebrity are alluring. People are drawn to those who walk in fame's spotlight, whether they are known for great accomplishments or for notorious deeds. The lives of the famous pique public interest and attract attention, perhaps because their experiences seem in some ways so different from, yet in other ways so similar to, our own.

Newspapers, magazines, and television regularly capitalize on this fascination with celebrity by running profiles of famous people. For example, television programs such as *Entertainment Tonight* devote all of their programming to stories about entertainment and entertainers. Magazines such as *People* fill their pages with stories of the private lives of famous people. Even newspapers, newsmagazines, and television news frequently delve into the lives of well-known personalities. Despite the number of articles and programs, few provide more than a superficial glimpse at their subjects.

Lucent's People in the News series offers young readers a deeper look into the lives of today's newsmakers, the influences that have shaped them, and the impact they have had in their fields of endeavor and on other people's lives. The subjects of the series hail from many disciplines and walks of life. They include authors, musicians, athletes, political leaders, entertainers, entrepreneurs, and others who have made a mark on modern life and who, in many cases, will continue to do so for years to come.

These biographies are more than factual chronicles. Each book emphasizes the contributions, accomplishments, or deeds that have brought fame or notoriety to the individual and shows how that person has influenced modern life. Authors portray their subjects in a realistic, unsentimental light. For example, Bill Gates— the cofounder and chief executive officer of the software giant Microsoft—has been instrumental in making personal computers the most vital tool of the modern age. Few dispute his business savvy, his perseverance, or his technical expertise, yet critics say he is ruthless in his dealings with competitors and driven more by his desire to maintain Microsoft's dominance in the computer industry than by an interest in furthering technology.

In these books, young readers will encounter inspiring stories about real people who achieved success despite enormous obstacles. Oprah Winfrey—the most powerful, most watched, and wealthiest woman on television today—spent the first six years of her life in the care of her grandparents while her unwed mother sought work and a better life elsewhere. Her adolescence was colored by promiscuity, pregnancy at age fourteen, rape, and sexual abuse.

Each author documents and supports his or her work with an array of primary and secondary source quotations taken from diaries, letters, speeches, and interviews. All quotes are footnoted to show readers exactly how and where biographers derive their information and provide guidance for further research. The quotations enliven the text by giving readers eyewitness views of the life and accomplishments of each person covered in the People in the News series.

In addition, each book in the series includes photographs, annotated bibliographies, timelines, and comprehensive indexes. For both the casual reader and the student researcher, the People in the News series offers insight into the lives of today's newsmakers—people who shape the way we live, work, and play in the modern age.

Variations on a Powerful Theme

If the greatest actresses in movie history have one thing in common, it is the ability to convey certain character traits not unlike their own, working within recurring themes to create film personalities that resonate with audiences.

Before Hilary Swank was born, legendary star Bette Davis enthralled audiences in film after film with her portrayal of flawed women desperate to rise above difficult situations. More recently, Julia Roberts has been successful playing women who appear self-reliant on the outside but are forced by circumstance to expose their vulnerable inner selves.

Add to this short but impressive list of great actresses the name of Hilary Swank. In a remarkably short time, Swank has found her niche in films by portraying characters in the grip of a powerful struggle. Her characters—no matter what the situation—all cling to the idea of holding true to and striving to obtain a lifelong goal. In such films as *Boys Don't Cry, The Affair of the Necklace, Iron-Jawed Angels, Million Dollar Baby*, and *Freedom Writers*, her characters have all been bonded by this common theme.

By staying true to their dream, her characters do not necessarily reap the rewards of success. There is great conflict and struggle in attempting to reach a goal, and that achievement may result in tragedy. Swank conveys this theme so successfully because it is a theme that exists strongly in her own life. Born into near poverty, she developed a strong sense of self-determination and discipline that has taken her out of an unhappy childhood and into the realm of multimillion-dollar film star.

Her mother taught her early on through example that she was capable of achieving any goal she set her mind on if she just worked hard at it. A strong personal code of ethics, combined with Hilary Swank's fertile and creative mind, is behind the characters she so memorably brings to life. Consequently, audiences and critics alike are astounded by her ability not to merely play a role but to seem to inhabit it.

Reflecting many of the same traits of the characters she inhabits, Hilary Swank will go to amazing lengths to make her portrayal more believable. For *Boys Don't Cry*, she lived as a man for almost a month to understand what her character went through. Her adoption of rigid personal habits and intense physical training to play a boxer in *Million Dollar Baby* paid off in a well-toned physique that believably conveyed the athletic prowess of her character.

Seen in a movie still from the film **Boys Don't Cry***,* **Hilary Swank (center)***,* **played a woman who posed as a man.**

Once she has inhabited the character and created its goal—the character's repeated theme of striving for a dream at any cost—she then takes her audience through some often unpopular ideas and concepts. Her films have dealt with such controversial issues as sexual identity crisis, hate crimes, women's rights, apartheid, and domestic violence.

By playing her parts so well that her fans are always eager to see her in another story, she has achieved the flexibility to explore variations on her theme, which expands and becomes more complicated as she matures. The variations on this potent theme have allowed Hilary Swank to carve a lasting place among an elite group of great women in film.

Chapter 1

Trailer Park Dreams

When Hilary Swank received her second Academy Award in 2005, she said that she was just a girl from a trailer park who had a dream. The dream that began in a trailer park was shaped by her childhood experiences and nurtured by her extremely supportive and devoted mother.

Early Traits

Hilary's mother, Judy, had her own dream, that of becoming a professional tap dancer. She did indeed work for a while as a dancer, but when she met and married Stephen Swank, her life took a turn away from her dreams. Pregnant with their first child at the age of nineteen, Judy began working as a secretary, while her husband trained in the Air National Guard. After the birth of their first child, a son named Daniel, Judy kept working and was promoted to executive secretary.

Eight years later, on July 30, 1974, Judy gave birth to Hilary Ann Swank in Lincoln, Nebraska. According to Judy, at a very early age her daughter exhibited the traits that would contribute to her adult acting career. "Even when she was a baby, she would sit and seriously watch people," recalled Judy. "Compared to her brother, who would smile at the bend of an elbow, Hilary would just watch."[1]

The reason for Hilary's shy but observational demeanor had much to do with her environment. Judy and Stephen Swank tried

Judy Swank, pictured with her daughter at the 2005 Screen Actors Guild Awards, says she taught Hilary that she could achieve almost anything through hard work and determination.

to make the marriage work, but problems developed that, to this day, Hilary will not talk about in detail. Since her brother was eight years older and both her parents worked, the young Hilary spent a good deal of time alone with her thoughts and dreams. Early on, she would often focus on one goal until she could realize its completion, such as catching a frog or climbing a challenging tree. When she was five years old, her mother watched in amazement as Hilary conquered a neighborhood tree. "[The tree] was probably 40 feet [(12m)] tall, and she cleared the top where it was swaying in the wind," recalled her mother. "It was part of that adventuresome spirit. If she feels it, she's not afraid to step forward. She's not a pull-her-foot-back kind of girl."[2]

A New Environment, a Troubled Family

When Hilary was six years old, her adventuresome spirit was put to the ultimate test. Her father requested a transfer to Washington State. Located ninety miles north of Seattle and an hour south of Vancouver, British Columbia, Bellingham is the last port city before the Washington coastline meets the Canadian border.

Since the National Guard only required a portion of Stephen Swank's time, he found additional work as a trailer park salesman. This allowed the Swanks to live in one of the park's trailers, with Judy Swank still working as an executive secretary. For Hilary, this new environment and her parents' ongoing problems meant even more time alone, forcing the young girl to spend an inordinate amount of time with her thoughts and dreams. "There are things about my childhood that I regret . . . and I think that my brother regrets," she reflected years later, "which is that my parents were so troubled in their relationship, that we were kind of neglected at times. . . . Ultimately, my parents did the best they could."[3]

Her Best Friend

The trailer park the Swanks lived in had one saving grace for young Hilary. The park was within walking distance of a dock that sat on Lake Samish, and Hilary spent every moment she possibly could on the dock or in the water. "Now, this is not just a beautiful body of water," she recalled, "it is one of my best friends. I say that because I shared all of my dreams, desires, happiness, fears and sadness—and every waking minute I could—with it."[4]

Hilary's love of Lake Samish was enhanced by the lush rain forest foliage that shielded her from the harsh realities of her life. Being on the lower economic scale in the small town made it hard for Hilary to make close friends in school. Her parents' marital woes and her lack or friends seemed a million miles away as she floated and dreamed in the crystal clear water. On Lake Samish she was far away from such concerns and dreamed of becoming an astronaut or an Olympic athlete.

"Hilary! Stop Staring"

Whether Hilary was in school or at the lake, a trait from infancy carried over into childhood and remained all the years of her life: She could not stop observing the behavior of other people. Her fascination with human behavior would become an important asset as an actor, but as a child it proved quite annoying. "I remember sitting at McDonald's and watching this man eat," recalled Swank. "I counted how many times he chewed his burger, watched the way he sipped his Coke and copied how he dipped his french fries in the ketchup. My mom had to elbow me: 'Hilary! Stop staring.' She repeated that demand a lot throughout my childhood. It was pretty much her mantra."[5]

When Hilary was in school or the YMCA day care in the summer, her lower income background, coupled with a natural shyness, made it difficult to make many friends. She begged her parents every Christmas and every birthday for a dog or cat to keep her company but was turned down at each request because of the trailer park restrictions on pets. When the trailer park came under new management, the restriction was lifted, and Hilary became the owner of a black Labrador she named Buddy. Buddy became her constant companion at the lake and shared her secret dreams of future greatness.

As a child, Swank found solace at a lake near the trailer park where her family lived.

Coming Alive

In school, Hilary excelled in athletics but found class work uninspiring. In 1983, when Hilary was nine, her mother encouraged her to audition for the Bellingham Theater Guild production of *The Jungle Book*. Judy Swank thought the famous Rudyard Kipling tale of a young boy named Mowgli who is raised by the animals of the jungle would help bring her daughter out of her shell. Hilary's curiosity and love

In a 1906 illustration from The Jungle Book, *Mowgli holds up the hide of the ferocious tiger Shere Khan. Young Swank played the boy Mowgli in a local theater production.*

of animals piqued her interest in the play, so she signed up to try out for the role of Bhageera, the black panther.

She auditioned for the role and waited impatiently to hear how she fared. The director, Mr. Pittis, approached Hilary, put his arm around her, and calmly asked her how she would feel about playing the lead role of Mowgli. The young girl was disheartened not to get the role she had wanted and even more disappointed over the prospect of playing a boy. Mr. Pittis convinced her to reconsider, and the end result changed the young girl's life. "We only did one performance but even now it's hard to express what it felt like," she said years later. "It was like coming alive, like suddenly knowing you're doing what you're supposed to be doing. It made me feel like I found a place . . . like I wasn't alone anymore."[6]

Hilary Swank now had a new dream to explore at the lake. Her dreams of being an astronaut were dashed when she heard that straight As in science were required. From the moment she performed in *The Jungle Book* as the young boy named Mowgli, Hilary Swank had no other dream than that of becoming a professional actor.

Junior Olympics

Her parents greeted Hilary's dream of theatrical greatness kindly since she was still only nine years old. They naturally assumed she might find something else of interest before she came of age, but they did not count on the young girl's fierce determination. Like the tree she climbed when she was five, acting became a goal she would conquer with her unflagging adventuresome spirit.

Since theatrical productions were not plentiful in Bellingham outside of the theater guild, Hilary also pursued other activities. Her early love of sports got her involved in both swimming and gymnastics. These competitive team sports, which also relied heavily on individual achievement, helped her hone skills of mental determination as well as learn how to push her body's physical endurance. Both of these important life skills would become great assets to her in adult life. She entered Washington State's Junior Olympics competition and was eventually ranked fifth of the state's all-around gymnasts. It was no small feat, but one that would not overshadow the young athlete's dreams of becoming an actor.

Unfortunately for Hilary, her dreams could no longer be shared with one of her few close friends. The trailer park again came under new ownership, which resurrected the no-pets ban of the original owners. Twelve-year-old Hilary was told by her parents that she could no longer keep Buddy. She tried in vain to keep her best friend but was told in no uncertain terms that a rule was a rule and she must abide by it. Saying good-bye to Buddy nurtured her growing sense of nonconformity, and for Hilary Swank, blind adherence to rules that did not have an acceptable logic to them became something she would always fight against.

Trailer Park Girl

As a young teen, Hilary became more sociable than she had been in grade school. Junior high and high school, which were more cliquish than grade school, found Hilary eventually making the acquaintance of several of the fellow students who lived nearby. She still spent time on Lake Samish, but now spent time in the homes of her classmates after school as well.

It was then that the difference between her economic standing and that of her classmates became solidified. Growing up in a trailer park carried with it a stigma of being lower class, and Hilary was reminded of it regularly when she visited the homes of her friends. Their homes were more ornate, and they also had the money to buy the latest fashionable clothing. Like any young girl, Hilary wanted those things for herself, but she did not hold it against her parents for not being able to provide them. She simply understood that she was different and struggled to accept her place in the world.

Keeping the Dream Alive

In spite of the unhappy events of her early years, Hilary's outlook remained surprisingly upbeat. She never seemed to let negative

The Letter

One event in Hilary Swank's early years that has remained burned in her consciousness took place on the last day of her eighth-grade year. While putting her books in her locker, Hilary felt something hit her lightly on the back of her head. She turned and saw a bunch of her friends running away and giggling, while at her feet was a wadded piece of paper. Late for class, she grabbed the paper, put it away, and did not look at it again until the end of the day. Hilary remembered the contents even years later: ". . . I got on the school bus and I opened up that letter, and it said, 'You think you're so cool, but you're not; you think you're so pretty, but you're ugly; you think you're so talented, but you suck.' I was heartbroken. I still can't figure it out. I don't think I did anything to deserve it."

Ingrid Sischy, "SWANK!" *Interview,* April 2000, p. 136.

experiences overwhelm her dreams and future plans. She firmly believed a better life awaited her outside the confines of the Bellingham trailer park.

Hilary's biggest supporter in realizing her dreams was, and remains to this day, her mother, Judy. She instilled in her daughter a strong sense that if something was wanted badly enough, then hard work and single-minded determination would help attain it. No matter what financial or emotional hardship Judy Swank had to deal with, nothing was more important to her than her family. Her personal dreams of being a dancer may not have come to fruition, but she made sure that her children never wanted for anything if she could help it. This example sent a powerful message to Hilary. "I had friends who had big houses on the lake nearby, but I never felt poor," recalled Hilary. "My mom would go into debt before I couldn't eat or my socks got holes."[7] Her mother's devotion was a lesson by example that Hilary carried with her throughout her childhood and beyond.

High School

Judy Swank's life lessons for her daughter were needed more than ever when Hilary entered Sehome High School. She competed in sports as an outlet for her energy and performed in plays when productions in Bellingham existed, but schoolwork still failed to inspire the young teenager.

Not all of Hilary's early experiences were uninspiring. She was greatly encouraged by earning the best junior actress award from the Bellingham Theater Guild for performing in such plays as Neil Simon's nostalgic comedy *Brighton Beach Memoirs*.

The month after Hilary turned fourteen, she was one of a group of students from her hometown, as well as the nearby Seattle area, to take a trip to Hollywood. Having been a tap dancer when she was younger, Judy Swank encouraged her daughter to go, and the result of the month-long trip would have influential repercussions in both of their lives.

The theater guild award and the trip to Hollywood only reinforced for Hilary that being an actor was her life's goal. Acting also ignited her curiosity in a way school never could, as she explained: "Everyone has their own story, and those stories are fascinating to me. So when I play a character, I get a kick out of figuring out what makes them tick—what they love, what brings them joy, all the little details that make them who they are. Even as a kid I was fascinated by people."[8]

Crossroads

Hilary's fascination with human behavior and her love affair with acting would soon receive an unexpected jolt of encouragement. Her parents' relationship continued to deteriorate, with several trial separations attempted over the years. Hilary had never been especially close to her father, and as she reached maturity, she became even closer to her mother. By the time Hilary was fifteen and in her sophomore year, she and her mother would be forced by circumstances to become the most important people in each other's lives.

The trial separations of Stephen and Judy Swank took their toll on everyone involved, and eventually the bond between them

A visit to Hollywood (pictured) with a group of students reinforced Swank's desire to be an actress.

frayed to the breaking point. Around this same time, Judy Swank was fired from her job as an executive secretary, forcing her to make a life-altering decision. She gave a great deal of thought to the crossroad her life had reached. Ultimately, she decided to include Hilary in her plans. "My mom said to me that I could do anything I wanted in life," recalled Hilary. "It still makes me very emotional because I just never questioned it. She just always believed in me."[9]

What Judy Swank believed in was her daughter's undeniable talent as an actor. Even more impressive was Hilary's steely determination to accomplish her goals, for she had proven time and again that she was willing to defy convention and achieve what she wanted in spite of the odds. Judy Swank informed her daughter that if she really wanted to act, then she should trust her instincts and turn her dream into reality. Putting her belief

When She Was Seventeen

In 2002 Hilary Swank filled in a questionnaire for *Seventeen* that asked what she was like when she was a teenager:

The best thing about being 17: The excitement of knowing the whole world was ahead of me.

I was always in my room lip-synching: to Tiffany. My brother would just cringe when I listened to her. I was also into Debbie Gibson, but I really liked AC/DC and Pearl Jam, too.

My favorite movies were: *Pretty in Pink* and *The Breakfast Club.*

In my bedroom: I had posters of Michael Jackson and *Growing Pains'* Kirk Cameron.

My high school boyfriend: Shane. He was my first real boyfriend. I don't think I treated him very well. I really cared about him, and now I regret that I was so mean to him. I've tried to find him since to tell him I'm sorry, but I haven't succeeded.

My closet was filled: with clothes from Esprit. I didn't have a lot of money growing up, so going to Esprit was a big splurge. I would buy whatever was on sale. I'd try to get a whole outfit if I could—from the headband all the way to the socks.

Hilary Swank, "When I Was 17," *Seventeen*, December 2002, p. 174.

into action, Judy Swank told Hilary that they were going to take seventy-five dollars in cash, a Mobil gas card, and any other minimal possessions they could and go to Hollywood to make Hilary's dream of becoming an actor a reality. Hilary recalled, "She said to me, 'If you want to pursue this dream, let's go.' So, we packed our suitcases, got in a car . . . I think it was an Oldsmobile Supreme, and drove."[10]

Judy Swank once more proved to her daughter that actions speak louder than words. Together they decided to leave behind their world in Bellingham and venture to the new world of Hollywood in the Oldsmobile they had purchased from a family member. Daniel and Stephen Swank stayed in Washington. Hilary Swank, just short of her sixteenth birthday, had walked away from a traumatic childhood, setting off with her mother at the wheel to a new life in Hollywood, California.

Chapter 2

The Art of Persistence

When Hilary and her mother moved to California in 1990, they had no clear plan for launching an acting career. Moreover, their chances of success in the extremely competitive field were small. Worse yet, the Swanks had no visible means of support, and Hilary was now a high school dropout. All they had was a dream. Through single-minded persistence and an unwavering belief in Hilary's ability to succeed, they moved south, hoping that Hilary would be able to achieve some level of success in the challenging new world of professional acting.

Living in an Oldsmobile

When the Swanks arrived in California, they not only lacked a plan of action but a place to stay as well. Severely limited in their options, Hilary and her mother lived in their car their first few days in Hollywood. "I didn't see it as anything sad or bad," recalled Hilary. "I was about to live my dream. I'm sure my mom was freaked out."[11]

Luckily for the Swanks, when Hilary had visited California the previous summer, she had made friends with a girl who lived in South Pasadena. A few days after arriving in California, Hilary was able to make contact with her friend at a most opportune time. The other girl's family was in the process of selling their home, and they negotiated an interesting plan for the Swanks. Hilary and her mother could use the house overnight for free as long as they were out in the morning before the real estate agent arrived to show the house to prospective buyers. The downside of this plan was that there was no electricity or furniture, requiring the Swanks to read by candlelight and sleep on air mattresses.

The first few mornings in Hollywood for the Swanks were spent in a controlled routine. They would wake up early, deflate their air mattresses, fold them up, and bring their possessions out to the car. They then drove to the nearest Denny's restaurant to share a Grand Slam breakfast of two eggs, two slices of bacon, two sausages, and two pancakes for the economical sum of $3.99. They would then get gas for the car on their Mobil gas card as well as any necessary supplies provided at the gas station's convenience store.

After moving to Hollywood, Swank and her mother—like this family—were reduced to living in their car for a short time.

Finding a Game Plan

With a precarious living situation in place, Hilary and her mother then went about finding out how to become a working actor in Hollywood. The Swanks quickly learned that an agent was needed to line up auditions for acting jobs. A portion of their small bankroll was used to purchase a book that gave the listing information for all the agents representing young talent. Judy Swank then began calling them from a phone booth while Hilary waited in the car.

Each call garnered more information about what the Swanks needed as Judy continued to contact each agency in hopes of getting her daughter signed as a client. They were told to get a résumé together, have eight-by-ten-inch glossy head-shot photos taken of Hilary, and get a telephone for callbacks, all of which cost more money than they had access to. Undaunted, Judy Swank kept making calls until she literally hit gold. "My mom, she's amazing," recalled Hilary. "She'd say, 'My daughter's beautiful and really talented. You should meet her.' I remember going into Harry Gold, that's the agency. They had me read a McDonald's commercial and then they signed me, just like that."[12]

Preparation Meets Opportunity

For Hilary Swank, whose formal training was admittedly limited, every experience was a learning one. "A teacher of mine once said the definition of luck is when preparation meets opportunity," said Swank. "I've always been a hard worker, I'm always trying to be better—better as a person, better at my art. And I really like to work. But I also think luck played a part."[13]

Having been lucky enough to be signed by the Gold Agency, Hilary began a round of auditions. Judy Swank would wait in the car and read a book while her daughter went in to do a reading. It was rough going at first, but very quickly Hilary adapted to the new challenge. "At auditions, I never saw the other people in the room as competition," she recalled. "I only saw the opportunity to get a job and learn and grow. Though I don't want to paint a purely happy-go-lucky picture . . . there were times when I would get tired of auditioning and question why I didn't get a certain job."[14]

Growing Pains Reunion

Newsweek magazine printed a discussion with several Oscar hopefuls for their January 23, 2005, issue. The following is the article's introduction as well as a humorous transaction that took place between *Growing Pains* alumni Hilary Swank and Leonardo DiCaprio. Swank was nominated for *Million Dollar Baby*, and DiCaprio was nominated for his performance in *The Aviator*.

A young Leonardo DiCaprio (left) appears with Kirk Cameron in a scene from Growing Pains.

On January 15, we gathered the most celebrated actors of the season for an intimate talk about the pains and joys of a life in pictures [including Paul Giamatti, Jamie Foxx, Kate Winslett and Annette Bening]. Leonardo DiCaprio, starring as Howard Hughes in Martin Scorsese's "The Aviator," joked around with Hilary Swank, who's another old friend, doing strange handshakes and calling her "homey." Then, for two hours, the acclaimed group discussed everything from how shoes shape a performance to why getting fired is a good thing.

Leo, don't you and Hilary have some past connection?

[LEONARDO] DICAPRIO: We knew each other when we were 15. We did a TV show together, "Growing Pains."

HILARY SWANK: It was actually my first job. I pulled a bunny out of a hat and went, "Ta-da!"

DICAPRIO: She hasn't changed.

SWANK: It feels like it was yesterday.

Sean Smith and David Ansen, "Oscar Roundtable," *Newsweek*, January 23, 2005, p. 46.

Taking Care of Business

In less than a year, sixteen-year-old Hilary was working fairly regularly on TV, and her mother soon found work again as a secretary. This allowed them finally to move into a permanent dwelling, the Oakwood Apartments in Pasadena. Hilary also enrolled in mail-order courses, first through Pasadena High School and then later through Santa Monica Community College. Eventually, her persistence resulted in acquiring her General Equivalency Degree, or GED, which is the equivalent of a high school diploma.

The work Hilary was getting was mostly on TV sitcoms. A staple of TV from its inception, *sitcom* is a shortened term for "situation comedy," a type of show in which the humor is often derived from family situations. Hilary often played the daughter of the adult stars or neighborhood friend of their children. She appeared on a short-lived show entitled *Camp Wilder* as well as the shows *Harry and the Hendersons* and *Evening Shade*. She played a semirecurring character on the show *Growing Pains*, a favorite from her childhood. Also appearing periodically on the show was a young actor named Leonardo DiCaprio, who was represented by the same agent as Hilary and who became a good friend of the young actress.

Earning TV credits helped to make her résumé more impressive, but she quickly learned that greater prestige came from movie credits. She finally got her first film credit in 1992's *Buffy the Vampire Slayer*. She portrays Kimberly, one of the friends of the title character, and utters the memorable line: "Oh, that's so five minutes ago."[15]

The key difference between Hilary Swank and many of her contemporaries, who became bitter and cynical when the work sought did not come their way, lay in her ability to soak up every experience and learn from it. If she did not pass an audition, she tried to find out why and figure out how she could improve herself for the next one. She did not let a negative experience sour her outlook; she had the persistence to push on even when the future looked bleak.

The Next Karate Kid

Hilary's ability to draw on a wide range of talents came in handy when she auditioned for the role of Julie Pierce in the film *The*

The Title Says It All

The failure of *The Next Karate Kid* notwithstanding, Hilary Swank continued to find work in a series of TV movies with self-explanatory titles. She appears in such projects as *Cries Unheard: The Donna Yaklich Story* (1994) as the victim of an abusive parent; a similarly-themed project entitled *Terror in the Family* (1996); and *Dying to Belong* (1997) as a college student who is tortured during a sorority initiation. Of these and similar projects, the actor remained philosophical. She said, "I never looked down on anything that I got. Of course there were some awful movies-of-the-week. But I always looked at it as an opportunity to grow."

She also worked in several projects intended for theatrical release. She plays an independent young woman in the Stephen King horror movie sequel *Sometimes They Come Back . . . Again* (1996) and a grieving sister looking to avenge her murdered brother in *Kounterfeit* (1996), both of which went directly to video. She also plays a confused young wife whose parents are killed by her husband, who defends himself by claiming he was sleepwalking, in a TV movie called *The Sleepwalking Killer* (1997).

Swank does a high kick in a scene from The Next Karate Kid.

Alexandra Jacobs, "Hilary Goes Wild!" *Allure*, July 2005, p. 144.

Next Karate Kid. It is the fourth installment in a series about how the lessons acquired in martial arts can help a young person deal with personal problems. The original Karate Kid, played by Ralph Macchio, had moved on, but his mentor, Mr. Miyagi, played by veteran character actor Pat Morita, was still plying his wisdom, only this time the student was to be a young girl.

"Spirit and Sparkle"

Hilary auditioned along with five hundred other hopefuls and was one of six narrowed down for the final decision. The producers then had the girls watch a karate move, such as a spin kick, and asked each of them to repeat it. Hilary's background in sports and natural athletic ability paid off; she quickly absorbed the difficult maneuvers and won the lead role of Julie Pierce.

Costar Pat Morita saw something else in Hilary that the other half-dozen actors lacked: "They were all what the script called for. But there was a certain spirit and sparkle that Hilary had that made the choice easier. There's a certain look in her eyes—that beam of great sincerity. Hilary had a handle on it."[16]

At the 2000 Independent Spirit Awards, Hilary Swank and Chad Lowe laugh with reporters.

Rocket to Stardom?

Filming of *The Next Karate Kid* began in June 1993, and by the time the cameras began rolling, Hilary Swank was up to the task. At 5 feet 7 inches (1.7m), with long, flowing brown hair and a toned physique, Swank had trained extensively for the three weeks prior to the start of filming.

When the film was released the next year, its reception by audiences and critics was disappointing.*The Next Karate Kid* had a brief, unprofitable run, dashing Hilary's perceived chance for breakout success. "Everyone said: 'This is going to rocket you into space! You're going to be huge!' The whole experience was terrible," she said later. "The movie was in the theater for a few weeks and it was gone. But it really didn't hit until I was trying to get the next job. The label was on. She's the Next Karate Kid. . . . Where can you go from there?"[17] Where she went was back to work, persistently striving for greater recognition.

Enter Chad Lowe

It was during the time she was struggling for recognition that her life took yet another interesting and unexpected turn. Shortly after Swank's eighteenth birthday, Leonardo DiCaprio accompanied her to a celebrity party combining sports and show business stars sponsored by MTV. The star-studded event also included a young actor named Chad Lowe. "I saw her and saw our future in her eyes," said Lowe. "She had the most beautiful eyes I'd ever seen. They speak volumes about her character."[18]

Lowe, the younger brother of actor Rob Lowe and almost seven years older than Swank, had made a name for himself on the TV show *Life Goes On*. Playing a dying AIDS victim, the Ohio native won an Emmy Award in 1993 for his performance on the show. When he met Hilary Swank, he was so taken by the young actress that he struck up a conversation, and the two began seeing each other over the next several weeks.

For Hilary Swank, who had dated briefly in high school and had been seeing someone at the time she met Lowe, the actor's persistence proved quite jarring. Fiercely independent and devoted to her work, the presence of a significant other in her life was something she was not at all prepared for. The more they saw of each other, however, the more she realized how much they had in common and how right they were for each other.

Not Playing "the Girl"

Unlike Lowe, Swank's career had reached a ceiling that she could not seem to get beyond. Several appearances in feature films went nowhere, and in some cases were not even seen in theaters. She maintained a high priority in terms of the projects she sought, but casting directors told Hilary that her face had an unconventional look. More bluntly, Swank heard that her lips and forehead were too large—as a result of her appearance and a dearth of meaningful roles, high-profile projects were hard to come by. "I think I made a conscious effort at the beginning of my career to be taken seriously," she said. "I didn't want to be 'the girl.' Because how boring is that?"[19]

Although she succeeded in avoiding projects that cast her as the girlfriend of the lead male character, the projects she did work on proved to be less than inspiring. The only saving grace during this period was a project in which she was able to costar with boyfriend Chad Lowe and several other up-and-coming young stars. Entitled *Quiet Days in Hollywood* (1997) and also sent directly to video, the plot involves several episodic vignettes that are all connected to the sexual dalliances of the main characters. Swank plays an idealistic Hollywood prostitute enamored with a down-and-out movie star.

Learning from the Past

Each project Swank worked on was gaining her valuable experience, but her phone was not ringing off the hook with follow-up offers. Her greatest consolation during this slow period was her relationship with Chad Lowe, with whom she now shared a home in Pacific Palisades, California, just minutes away from where Judy Swank lived.

Although Swank had been leery of marriage, her relationship with husband Chad Lowe appears strong in this 2005 photo.

The two young actors had fallen in love, but Swank was understandably wary of marriage. Her parents had been unable to make their marriage work, and Lowe's parents had also divorced when he was an infant. Swank set down some important ground rules, such as premarital counseling, for the relationship to continue. She explained:

> We got engaged when I was 23, and our engagement year was probably the most difficult because we started to think about what marriage really meant to us. We both wanted marriage to mean forever. I'd watched my parents try to make [their marriage] work, but at a young age, even I could see it wasn't working—they were very different. Chad and I didn't want those little things that bug you about one another to become bigger once we got married. So we asked ourselves, "What is it in our perceptions of one another that needs to change?" There was a lot of give-and-take on both of our sides.[20]

Swank and Lowe married on October 2, 1997, and honeymooned in Hawaii.

Beverly Hills 90210

When Hilary Swank returned from her honeymoon, she plunged headlong into her acting career, moving on to a new agent who did not specialize in handling children or younger girls. This new agent wasted no time sending Swank out on auditions, one of which landed the young actor a well-paying job.

The TV show *Beverly Hills 90210* had been extremely popular in the early 1990s. The prime-time show centered on a Midwestern family's adjustment to life in the wealthy California suburb. It proved to be wildly successful among young teens, and the show's focus shifted from the Midwestern family to the young and good-looking cast. Over time, producer Aaron Spelling realized he could no longer maintain many of the characters' youthful circumstances and decided to have his writers create a character of a young single mother who was eventually to marry the character of Steve, played by popular actor Ian Ziering.

Hilary Swank's Menagerie

Ever since she was a child, Hilary Swank has loved animals. In *Interview* magazine, she explained the history of her still growing menagerie:

> When I first moved in with my husband Chad, I said to him, "Now that we're living together, there's one thing that you need to know: If I bring home an animal, that's just how it's going to be. There's not even going to be a discussion." And he was fine with this. About a month later, I bought an African gray parrot, which I named Seuss after Dr. Seuss, one of my favorite authors. . . . There's Lucky, my border-collie mix whom I saved from the pound. Just recently I got a cat named Deuce. . . . When I turned twenty-five I went to visit Chad, who was working in Northern California, and went into a barn and saw a bunny sitting there. . . . So when Chad asked what I wanted for my birthday, instead of this beautiful, thousand-dollar luggage set he had picked out, I was like, "No, no, I want this bunny." So he bought him. His name is Luna, and Luna is having a very happy life.

Alec Baldwin, "At Home with the Hottest Actress of the Moment—and Her Rainbow Tribe," *Interview*, June 2000, p. 87.

Hilary Swank auditioned for and won the role of single mother Carly Reynolds and was contracted for two seasons, beginning with the 1997–1998 season. "She was so sweet, so dear," said Spelling. "She has the greatest eyes; they tell you everything. I remember saying, after about her third show, 'I love her, she has a soul.'"[21]

The show was in its eighth season when Swank joined the cast and attempted to breathe some new life into the proceedings. Longtime watchers balked at the attempt and let their feelings be known in fan mail to the producers. By the sixteenth episode of

Swank appears in costume on the set of Beverly Hills 90210. *Her character was written out of the script shortly after she joined the cast.*

the season, Swank was called into Spelling's office and told that her character was being written out of the show. Spelling tried to console her by stating the fans of Ziering did not want to see him settle down, but she was inconsolable. "I honestly thought I needed to quit and find a new occupation. I broke down and cried in his office and at home,"[22] recalled Swank.

"Too Half-Hour"

Devastated by her dismissal from the cast of *Beverly Hills 90210*, Swank sank into the lowest time in her life. In spite of years of persistence and the support of her mother and her husband, Hilary Swank was for the first time beginning to doubt herself.

She continued to audition after leaving *90210*, focusing on dramatic hour-long TV programs, but without much luck. Swank recalled:

> I would hear that my forehead is too big, my lips are too big, my name is awful, that I wasn't a dramatic actress, that I have bad hair. For example, there was this role that I was dying to get, on an hour-long television pilot. When I tested for the role, the network execs said, "You're great, but you're just too 'half-hour' for this." I thought, well that's one opinion, and I kept auditioning for dramatic roles.[23]

Swank did indeed keep auditioning for one-hour dramatic shows and not the half-hour sitcoms that the executive suggested. Although after almost nine years of struggling she had not progressed to the point she had wanted to, Hilary Swank refused to relinquish her dream. Soon, having determined to stick it out, she would be rewarded with the chance of a lifetime.

Chapter 3

Dreams Do Come True

Leaving *Beverly Hills 90210* was a terrible blow to Hilary Swank. She received solace from friends and family, but she remained deeply upset by the experience. In spite of lacking formal training and not having conventional good looks, she had managed to get fairly steady work in the fiercely competitive field. Her natural ability and personal discipline saw her through the trying times, but, ironically, now that she had reached a point of being able to do work of greater depth, her career seemed to be stalled. A project was soon destined to come her way that would answer her prayers and result in one of the most highly regarded performances in movie history.

The Real Teena Brandon

There was no way Swank could have known, but a film was being prepared that would give her the opportunity she had been dreaming about. The project was based on the true story of Teena Renae Brandon, born in 1972 in the same Lincoln, Nebraska, hospital as Hilary Swank. Brandon was born a biological female but from the age of eighteen lived as a man.

Teena Brandon's father died in a car accident before she was born, and her teenaged mother struggled to make ends meet. Like

Swank, Brandon left high school before graduating but from that moment on went by a series of male aliases, including Billy Brinson, Charles Brayman, Brandon Yale, and others. Her dream was to have a sex-change operation someday, but until that could happen she would live her life as if she were a man. She also forged checks and ran up the credit cards of the girls she dated. She proved popular with some of the local girls, but whenever her true identity was discovered, Teena would spiral into depression. At nineteen she attempted suicide and spent time in a crisis center for therapy.

In November 1993, she tried to start life anew by moving to Falls River, Nebraska. It was while she was in Falls River that she

The life story of Teena Renae Brandon (pictured), who began living as a man in her late teens and died a violent death, was made into the film **Boys Don't Cry.**

met John Lotter and Tom Nissen, two violent ex-convicts who took a liking to the person they assumed was a young man. Brandon began dating Lotter's ex-girlfriend, Lana Tisdel, as well as another young girl who had just had a baby. On Christmas Eve, after they discovered her true gender, Lotter and Nissen raped and beat Teena Brandon. When the police ignored her pleas for protection, she fled to the nearby town of Humboldt, where, on New Year's Eve, twenty-one-year-old Teena Brandon and two others were beaten and murdered. Lotter and Nissen were convicted and sentenced, with Nissen serving a life sentence in exchange for testifying against Lotter, who is awaiting execution.

Kimberly Peirce

In 1994 the story of Teena Brandon, who was posthumously called Brandon Teena by the media, caught the attention of a young Columbia University film student, a former tomboy named Kimberly Peirce. Over the next several years, as Peirce was researching and developing the story of Brandon for a feature film, Hilary Swank was searching for a worthwhile project to display her ability. By the time Peirce had prepared a script for the Teena Brandon story, Swank had just been released from her *90210* contract. "Two weeks later, I got a call from my agent," recalled Swank. "She said, 'You have got to read this script, it is amazing.' It was *Boys Don't Cry.*"[24]

Peirce had auditioned several hundred actors out of her New York office but could not seem to find the one who could embody Teena Brandon's dream of wanting to be a man. Exhausted and frustrated, Peirce was watching a series of videotape auditions submitted by various agents when she came across Hilary Swank's. "She blew my mind," Peirce recalled. "It was clear this was someone who could make Brandon believable to audiences. That scene where Hilary puts on a cowboy hat and looks at herself allowed us to drop 10 pages of dialogue. We didn't have to explain this is someone posing as a boy. Her actions said it."[25] Most of all, the director saw that Swank genuinely understood Brandon's efforts to be a man.

Hilary Swank (left) is pictured in 2002 with writer/director Kimberly Peirce, who cast the actress in the challenging lead role in Boys Don't Cry.

Becoming Teena Brandon

Swank was told by her agent that the producers for *Boys Don't Cry* liked her video and suggested she go to New York for an interview. Instead of waiting to have the producers fly her out, Swank paid her own way to the audition. Before leaving, she delved into becoming Teena Brandon.

Swank's initial transformation was very involved. She called her grandfather in Nebraska, who told her all about the tragic, true story that made national headlines. She also contacted her father in Portland, Oregon, whom she used as a model for Brandon's masculine manners. By the time she arrived at Peirce's New York hotel dressed in her husband's clothes, she was so convincing as a man that the doorman did not immediately let Swank in for her appointment, since he was told a young girl and not a man was scheduled to meet the director.

Swank passed the audition and agreed to a strenuous preparation to further transform herself into Teena Brandon. The timing was such that her previous experiences had earned her the skills to approach the challenge. She was elated finally to earn a role that fulfilled her dream of challenging her acting talent. She also understood Brandon's dilemma more than any character she had played before. As an outsider in Bellingham, Swank identi-

Heartwood

Just before *Boys Don't Cry* came along, Swank was still desperately struggling for recognition. "It's like a Catch-22. In order to get the job you really want, you have to prove yourself but in order to prove yourself, you have to get the job," she said.

Her desperation resulted in her appearance in a film that never saw general release. *Heartwood* (1998) concerns a small Pacific Northwest logging community's attempts to stave off the takeover of a family-owned logging company by a cold and unfeeling banking corporation.

Swank plays Sylvia Orsini, who is the love interest to the film's main character, but she has more to do than simply bolster the hero. Her character is at a crossroads in her own life as to whether to return to school or help her new boyfriend deal with the logging company's dilemma. She then takes an active part in fending off the banking corporation. In one short scene, she and the male character are shown leaving a biker bar. None other than Swank's mother, Judy Swank, plays one of the more prominent bikers.

Randall King, "Looking for Mr. Right," *Canoe—Jam!* March 31, 2000. http://jam.canoe.ca/Movies/Artists/S/Swank_Hilary/2000/03/31/762111.html.

fied with Brandon's need to be accepted on her own terms, even referring to Brandon as a man during interviews. She said, "What drew me to Brandon was the sheer joy he had living his life the way he wanted to live it. When someone's living their dream, and not conforming to what society wants them to be, they exude joy. He loved to be a boy and I loved that he followed his dream and had the courage to be himself."[26]

Swank had almost a month to prepare herself physically and emotionally for the role. She agreed to cut her hair and lose enough weight that her strong jawbone and facial structure would be highlighted, making her appear more masculine. Since she would only be paid three thousand dollars for the part, she could not afford a speech coach to help her develop a Midwestern accent. Instead she contacted a cousin in Iowa. "I had my cousin Billy talk into a tape [recorder] for an hour. He picked up a Woolworth's ad saying, 'Oranges are on sale for one dollar and nahn-dee-nahn cents.' But God bless him, because it worked,"[27] she said.

Strap and Pack

To approach the more difficult task of transforming herself emotionally into Teena Brandon, Hilary Swank agreed to additional modifications to her body. As Brandon had done, she strapped down her breasts with an ace bandage and packed the front of her pants with a pair of socks.

Hilary Swank then went even further to connect emotionally with her character. She actually decided to live as a man by wearing her husband's clothes and passing herself off as a distant relative. Peirce encouraged the month-long prefilming experiment and told the actor not to let on who she really was even if it meant ridicule and embarrassment, so she could know what Brandon felt. "I don't think I was really prepared for what I went through," Swank said. "There were people who couldn't figure out what I was. They didn't look me in the eye. I was treated poorly by people in stores, people that I had known as Hilary. I cried for two days straight."[28]

The only aspect of the gender reversal left to conquer was the voice. Swank had mastered the accent but knew her voice was too high to sound believable as a teenage boy. Instead, she opted to speak her dialogue barely above a whisper, which would enable her to sound more boyish as well as know what Brandon had done to accomplish the same task. The fact that Swank could barely breathe with her breasts tightly strapped down aided the effort considerably.

Making *Boys Don't Cry*

With her intense and ongoing research to achieve her aim of making Teena Brandon a reality, Hilary Swank arrived on the Dallas set of *Boys Don't Cry* ready to commence filming. She did not socialize much with the rest of the cast, choosing instead to remain in character during production whether she was filming or not.

The film was made on a tight budget, and the shooting script was altered from real events to enhance the emotional impact of the story. Working collaboratively, the filmmakers chose not to include Brandon's mother in the story as well as several other characters, such as one of the murder victims found alongside Brandon. Instead, the film focused solely on Brandon's acceptance into the society of outcasts in Falls City, with greater emphasis placed on her relationship with Lana Tisdel.

Aspects of that relationship sometimes became a point of contention on the set. Since Brandon never saw herself as a homosexual but as a straight man who could love women, the filmmakers were occasionally at odds as to what the point of view in a scene should be. Ultimately, it was decided that those members of the project who were gay and had more experience with nonheterosexual situations would guide the straight members of the project.

This intense involvement by the major participants almost caused an altercation between the director and her star. Just before they were to shoot the scene in which the police interview Brandon after the rape, the director saw Swank doing something that seemed to have nothing to do with the scene. "She was listening to the Walkman," recalled Peirce. "I thought, 'Is she listening to music?' I turned to her and I just said, 'What are you doing?'

As this scene from the movie shows, Swank underwent an emotional and physical transformation in creating the character of Teena Brandon.

Hilary Swank on John Lotter

During an interview to promote *Boys Don't Cry*, Hilary Swank was caught off guard by a question concerning convicted killer John Lotter and reacted spontaneously:

> It's clear her emotional involvement in the story has not dulled when I point out that Lotter appears in the new Benetton campaign that features 50 Death Row prisoners. Swank is genuinely shocked, her eyes fill with tears and her voice breaks.

"Are you kidding? Are you f—ing kidding me? John Lotter? I think I'm going to throw up. I am so mad about that campaign. I think it's disgusting, it's vile. I don't usually get political but I think that's

In a 2000 photo, Teena Brandon's mother holds pictures of her daughter.

wrong. I will NEVER buy anything from Benetton. I just won't. What are they saying? That if you kill someone and you're on Death Row we'll put you in a magazine in some of our clothes?"

Perhaps they were just trying to make the condemned human?

"You don't humanize people by making them into models. If you want to teach people, 'don't do that,' put some money toward educating young kids who need help. Why don't they put their money there?"

Edward Helmore, "Based on a True Story," *Dazed and Confused*, April 2000, p. 67.

She took the earphone and put it in my ear and she was listening to Brandon's voice. It was just chilling."[29]

Unexpected Reactions

When filming on *Boys Don't Cry* was completed, Hilary Swank returned to California and tried to get Teena Brandon out of her system. It was weeks before the actor could feel like herself again, such was the way in which the character so effectively got under her skin.

Once postproduction was completed on the independently made film, it played at several U.S. and international film festivals in hopes of finding a distributor. The film proved to be a hit on the festival circuit, with Fox Searchlight Pictures agreeing to distribute the film in theaters.

When *Boys Don't Cry* was released in the fall of 1999, critics were unanimous in their praise. The director was heralded by critics for her vision in telling the controversial story of love, passion, bigotry, and hate. The one component that received uniform praise above all others was the performance of Hilary Swank. As the film award season began, Swank won virtually every major award for her performance, including best actress from the New York and Los Angeles film critics associations, the Independent Spirit Award, the MTV Movie Award, the National Board of Review, and the Golden Globe. The unprecedented string of accolades meant that Hilary Swank was no longer a struggling actor dreaming of the one great role that would prove her talent. Her dream had finally come true.

More than Critical Praise

Another reaction to her performance caught the young actor by surprise and profoundly affected her. People outside of the film community were responding to her performance. She received mail from people who stated that her performance changed their way of thinking from hating cross-gendered or gay people to beginning to be more understanding toward them. Swank found the ability to change people's way of thinking uplifting: "It's hard to explain, but that's what I want to do, to keep doing, as I keep growing into different roles."[30]

Not only had her performance changed the way some people had negatively looked upon the sexual orientation of some individuals, it brought emotional reactions from the victims of such negative treatment. Young people grappling with their sexual identity began contacting Swank and thanked her profusely for helping them find the courage to deal with their problems.

Swank was so moved that she became actively involved with New York's Hetrick-Martin Institute, created to help young people deal with their gender issues. "It's hard enough to go through life as a straight kid," reasoned Swank. "I remember being a teenager, and they were such hard years. To think of all the torment I got for not wearing the right pants or whatever. Then to imagine what they go through—it's so unfair."[31]

The Academy Awards

When Hilary Swank received word of yet another profound tribute to her work, she was in the midst of her next project. While filming *The Gift* in the swamps of Georgia, she learned that she had been nominated for an Academy Award for best actress in *Boys Don't Cry*.

On the night of March 26, 2000, Swank and her husband, Chad Lowe, sat nervously in the audience of the live broadcast of the Academy Awards. Her category was announced toward the end of the evening, and when the envelope was opened she was called to the stage. At twenty-five years old, she was one of the youngest actors to receive the prestigious award, and as she took the stage, both her gratitude and her nervousness were evident: attempting to thank everybody connected with her performance, she forgot to mention her husband.

The Life of an Actor

After her Academy Award victory, offers deluged her agent for future projects. By portraying Teena Brandon's tragic dream so effectively on-screen, Hilary Swank's own dream of creative

Jubilant, Swank displays her Golden Globe best actress award, one of many awards she garnered for her role in Boys Don't Cry.

Swank celebrates with her husband after winning the best actress Academy Award for Boys Don't Cry.

recognition had finally come true. The offers she was receiving included multimillion-dollar salaries for such projects as *The Silence of the Lambs* sequel and the Martin Scorsese project *Gangs of New York*. Ultimately other women played those roles, while Swank continued to search for the right follow-up project.

While considering what project she would do next, Swank dropped into a pharmacy and received a humorous reminder of how quickly her life had changed. Because she only earned three thousand dollars for *Boys Don't Cry,* she did not have health insurance from the Screen Actors Guild, which required a minimum of five thousand dollars a year and would have covered the cost of the prescription. "So, I had an Academy Award, and I didn't have health insurance," said Swank, laughing. "The life of an actor."[32]

Chapter 4

The Challenge of Success

Hilary Swank achieved the ultimate goal in a very competitive industry in a relatively short period of time. Having won an Oscar as well as many other honors for her performance in *Boys Don't Cry*, she was now faced with having to sustain that success. Admittedly at a loss over how to proceed with her career, she sought out projects that were creatively challenging but not necessarily geared for commercial success. Over the next several years, from this variety of projects, she learned more and more about herself and her craft.

The Gift

Swank's first film project after *Boys Don't Cry* was in production when she won the Academy Award. It was called *The Gift*, a thriller with an ensemble cast of talented actors overseen by cult director Sam Raimi. The story of a young widow, played by Cate Blanchett, who supports her family by means of the gift she has for telling fortunes, features a gruesome murder plot and a frightening conclusion. Swank has a relatively small role as one of Blanchett's clients, an abused wife named Valerie Barksdale, whose violent husband is played by Keanu Reeves. The cast also includes Greg Kinnear, Katie Holmes, and Giovanni Ribisi.

Grappling with the character's reasons for staying in an abusive relationship was yet another challenge for the actress. For Valerie Barksdale's background, Swank was able to draw on her memories of growing up in the Bellingham trailer park, where she witnessed domestic violence firsthand. To understand her character's mind-set, she sought the help of an abuse counselor. "At first I thought it would be so hard to play a woman who is abused because I would never let anyone touch me that way," she said. "What I realized was that Valerie would probably have been abused as a child and that abuse was a form of love to her."[33]

A minor obstacle developed when costar Reeves found it difficult to perform the physically demanding abuse on Swank that the script called for. As she had done with her costars before filming the graphically violent scenes in *Boys Don't Cry*, Swank took her fellow actor aside and gave Reeves permission for his character to do to her character what was needed. This reassurance

Following her Oscar win, Swank appears in a scene from
The Gift, a poorly received film.

went a long way in making the sequence much more frighteningly believable to the audience.

The film was released in 2000 but did not do especially well at the box office. However, Hilary Swank's small but poignant contribution earned her a best supporting actress nomination from the Science Fiction/Horror Movie Association.

Post-Oscar Planning

By the time *The Gift* was released, Hilary Swank had been named the best actress of 2000 by the Academy of Motion Picture Arts and Sciences and virtually every other film-related organization. She was deluged with offers for magazine interviews, TV appearances, and possible film projects. She also found it necessary to hire a small army of assistants to help deal with the offers and career moves she was planning, including fashion consultants, stylists, and publicists. Both the agent and the manager who had helped negotiate her appearance in *Boys Don't Cry* were replaced. Swank signed a new contract with Kevin Huvane, the powerful Creative Artists Agency executive who also represented Tom Cruise. "Every agent in town called me," she explained. "I met with everybody, but [CAA] seemed to have the best game plan."[34]

The game plan included her next project, which on the surface was as different from *Boys Don't Cry* and *The Gift* as she could have possibly imagined. It was called *The Affair of the Necklace* and was based on the life of Jeanne de la Motte-Valois. The little-known story concerns a French woman fighting to reclaim her family's land and title in eighteenth-century France. When her appeals through traditional channels fail, she concocts an elaborate scam against the country's most powerful people, including the cardinal of all France and Queen Marie Antoinette. "I'm somehow drawn to true stories," Swank said. "They say life is stranger than fiction. This is another amazing character who is so strong. But the movie is the polar opposite from 'Boys Don't Cry.' I get to have long hair and a beautiful wardrobe."[35]

Although the characters were otherwise completely dissimilar, both Teena Brandon and Jeanne de la Motte-Valois had pursued

Hilary Swank on Style and Beauty

After Hilary Swank became a major fashion icon through her stylish appearances on award shows, the United Kingdom edition of the fashion magazine *Elle* asked her opinion on style and beauty for their April 2005 issue:

Who do you think is beautiful? 'Kate Winslet has the most amazing face—it's so pretty, but it's also quite real. Meryl Streep is gorgeous—she has that intelligence in her face.'

Which women in Hollywood embody sex appeal? 'Salma Hayek because of her curves, her fire and fearlessness. Catherine Zeta-Jones is all woman; I loved the way she turned up to last year's Oscars full of her pregnancy. Annette Bening is incredibly sexy—she's confident and strong.'

Greatest beauty myth? 'That you have to be thin and flawless.'

Your favorite look? 'I love to have different looks.'

Favorite designers? 'Calvin Klein, Marc Jacobs.'

Secret Shop? 'Anthropologie in New York for great vintage.'

What's the best part of a woman's body? 'Any curve. It's what makes us different.'

Swank and one of her favorite designers, Calvin Klein, attend a fashion event together.

Louise Gannon, "Sexy Lady," *Elle* (UK), April 2005, p. 122.

Swank's character dupes France's powerful queen, Marie Antoinette (pictured), in **The Affair of the Necklace.**

a very specific dream, and neither would be deterred by the dangers along the way. "When all that you hold dear is taken," says Swank's character, Motte-Valois, "risk is of little consequence."[36] Swank, who herself was intensely focused on a dream, brought a special depth to her portrayal of these driven characters.

Learning the Role, Feeling the Pressure

The film's director, Charles Shyer, had met with Swank before seeing her in *Boys Don't Cry* and felt that she was personable enough. When he saw her Oscar-winning performance, he was relieved to discover she could also act.

In **The Affair of the Neck-lace,** *Swank and her costars donned the elegant clothing of the period.*

Once signed on to the *Necklace* project, Swank again wasted no time researching her part, reading historical books and consulting with experts who could help her better understand her character. She sought out a University of California, Los Angeles, professor who specialized in eighteenth-century etiquette so she could walk and carry herself appropriately.

Two weeks after the Academy Awards, with production of the new film about to begin, Swank and director Shyer left California. Shyer was slightly apprehensive about his leading lady, who had so convincingly played Teena Brandon. "We went to Rome to meet with [costume designer] Milena Canonero, and Hilary went in to try on her hair and makeup," recalled Shyer. "When I walked in and saw her in this wig, I was just completely swept away—when she turned around, she had immediately stepped into the 18th century. It was such a relief."[37]

Swank, however, was beset by anxiety during the making of the film, noting that early on she had felt intense pressure to succeed. Close associates remarked on the star's problems as well. Her *Boys Don't Cry* director, Kimberly Peirce, noted that Swank may have been too contemporary a presence to carry off a costume piece like *Affair of the Necklace*. Perhaps audiences agreed with Peirce's assessment, since the film did not do well at the box office when it was released in 2001.

Becoming a New Yorker

Before the release of *The Affair of the Necklace*, Swank continued her search for worthwhile films. The offers were plentiful now that she was a known entity in the film industry, but Swank was more interested in a project's creative challenge rather than its chances of financial success.

To help her decide what project to do next, she and her husband decided to leave Los Angeles and move to New York. The decision was partly based on the fact that Swank felt creatively insulated and wanted to be in a culturally diverse environment. They rented an apartment in lower Manhattan in December 2000 and began to fit in almost immediately. "I love this city. I love it culturally," she said. "I feel like I'm in a blender of life. I ride the subway. I walk around the city all the time."[38]

In their new surroundings, Swank and her husband wasted no time making a home for themselves. They entertained close friends, made space for their growing menagerie of pets, and in no time at all, fit right into their adopted neighborhood.

The new lifestyle was jarred by the events of September 11, 2001. The terrorist attack on the World Trade Center occurred

The Concert for New York City

Hilary Swank took part in the concert held in Madison Square Garden to honor those who risked their lives on 9/11. She came onstage with a paramedic and his son to help introduce Five for Fighting:

> Hilary Swank: I have here Earl Holland and his son Andrew. He's a paramedic and on a September afternoon, on the way home from a memorial service honoring four colleagues lost in the tragedy, Earl Holland turned on his car radio. The group Five for Fighting happened to be on and they were singing their hit "Superman." The lyrics hit home and Earl decided to contact the group. He wrote, "Your song brought tears to my eyes. The lost rescuers were just everyday people with families but they were Supermen trying in vain to save others. So, if it's not too much to ask, during your travels or during a concert, if you could dedicate this song to my friends and to all the Supermen of this world, they would indeed be proud." Earl, you made it happen. This moment is yours.

> Earl: So, to all my friends, and those who gave their lives, here is their anthem, "Superman" [by] Five for Fighting.

The Concert for New York City, DVD, directed by Louis J. Horvitz. New York: Columbia Music Video, 2001, disc 2, cut 24.

Swank appears with screen legend Al Pacino in a scene from the dark thriller Insomnia.

just a short subway ride from where Swank lived, and she wasted no time volunteering her services. A lifelong lover of animals, she helped set up a neighborhood shelter for strays as well as getting involved in other community organizations. "After September 11, I felt like I was officially a New Yorker," said Swank. "I was here and was part of that community when it happened. Everyone came together and that didn't surprise me. That was one of the reasons why I moved here—the community of people."[39]

Working with an Icon

When the dust settled on the events of 9/11, Hilary Swank was still without a new project to work on. After much consideration and the failure of *Necklace* to connect with audiences, she decided on a much more contemporary film. Film icon Al Pacino was cast as the lead, a Los Angeles detective sent to Alaska to investigate a murder. Director Christopher Nolan's film is called *Insomnia*, and the detective suffers from the title ailment due to his involvement in a murder as well as his difficulty sleeping during Alaska's six months of daylight.

Pacino had been a major film star since the 1970s, with such films as *The Godfather* (1972), *Serpico* (1973), and *Scarface* (1983) to his credit. Casting Pacino in *Insomnia* created interest for other actors. "It opened the floodgates of casting possibilities. Every actor wants to be part of an Al Pacino movie,"[40] said Nolan. One such actor was Hilary Swank, who agreed to play a smaller part in the film.

The chance to work with Al Pacino was an opportunity Swank reveled in. Aiding her enthusiasm for the project was the character she played, a young detective named Ellie Burr. Like Swank herself, Burr wants to excel at her chosen profession. The rookie officer idolizes Pacino and does whatever she can to help the beleaguered police veteran. Swank said: "For an actor to be able to work with someone like that is something we dream about. Those qualities are exactly what Ellie Burr feels for [Pacino's character] Will Dorma. I got away with being as observant as I wanted to be, which was fantastic."[41]

Swank managed to carve her own niche in the complicated film in spite of the presence of Pacino and another very famous costar, Robin Williams, who played the pursued murderer. In her smaller role, Swank contributed a portrait of the transformation of Ellie Burr from rookie cop to investigative detective. Her famous ability to research a role and get under a character's skin was done slightly differently for this project. "She's a rookie detective when the film starts, and I didn't want to be knowledgeable and comfortable in that situation," said Swank. "So, one of the things I didn't do is go and hang out with detectives and feel that out. I wanted it to feel very new and very fresh."[42]

Back-to-Back

Since *Insomnia* was filmed mostly in Vancouver, British Columbia, Swank had a rare opportunity to visit nearby Bellingham. Accompanying her on the trip was her husband. They traveled to many of the spots Swank knew from her childhood, including the dock on

Lake Samish where she had dreamed of her future. With her dog Buddy no longer at her side, she plunged into the ice-cold water with her new best friend—her husband, Chad Lowe.

The respite was short-lived as Swank went directly into her next project, which was also set to be filmed in Vancouver. "It's one of the few times I did films back-to-back," she said. "I prefer to do one movie a year. I don't know how some actors do five pictures a year. I couldn't walk, let alone act, if I tried that."[43]

The project, scheduled for release in 2003, was yet another departure from what she had done up to that point. In an effort to continually challenge herself and not do what was expected of her, Hilary Swank agreed to star in the science-fiction film *The Core*. The plot requires an elite group of experts to travel to the inner core of the earth in a dangerous last-ditch effort to accelerate its slowing rotation.

The character of Rebecca Childs, like other women Swank had portrayed, has a single-minded determination to realize a goal. In this instance, the goal is to be a NASA astronaut, something Swank had considered herself in early childhood, and she played the part accordingly. "I felt that this character was more like me than anyone I have ever played before," she said. "I didn't condescend in any way, I played it totally straight. You know why? Because in my imagination, being an astronaut is something that I dreamed of. So I wasn't going to blow the one chance I had!"[44]

As she had always done in the past, Swank researched her character diligently and even based much of her performance on the model provided by Susan Helms, a real-life space station astronaut who advised the actor during the film.

Regrettable Timing

In an unfortunate coincidence, *The Core* was released just months after the mission of the space shuttle *Columbia* had ended in disaster. A chilling fictional reentry into the earth's atmosphere opens *The Core*, with Hilary Swank avoiding a *Columbia*-like catastrophe by landing her craft in the Los Angeles flood-control system. The spectacular sequence had been used in coming attractions, but the trailer was pulled from theaters after the *Columbia* disaster. Paramount Pictures thought it too exploitative to advertise their film in such a manner. By the time the film was released in March 2003, almost no one went to see it.

Trying to Work a *Miracle*

While *The Core* was doing lackluster business in theaters, Hilary Swank was already involved in her next project. Always interested in doing something new and challenging, she never overlooked the possibility of acting in live theater, as she had done as a child. One of her all-time favorite films was *The Miracle Worker* (1962), the story of near-blind Annie Sullivan's attempts to teach the deaf and blind young Helen Keller how to communicate. When Swank was approached to star in a revival of the original play with plans to go to Broadway, she happily took on the role of Sullivan.

Playing an astronaut in the science fiction film The Core, *Swank appears in a tense scene with Aaron Eckhart.*

After The Core *received a lukewarm reception and Swank's plans for a stage production of* The Miracle Worker *fizzled, critics began questioning her project choices.*

The play went through out-of-town tryouts in North Carolina, but early critical reaction was overwhelmingly negative. The original director left over creative differences with the producer, who in turn could not seem to raise the additional funding needed to take the production to Broadway. The project folded before it could reach New York, sending Hilary Swank in search of other worthwhile projects.

The lack of success of Swank's last few projects had several people giving her public advice. Casting director Felicia Fasano, in a letter to the *New York Times*, suggested that some of Swank's more recent projects were poorly chosen and counseled the star to play superheroes or romantic interests, like other well-known stars. Swank responded:

> I think it's great that I'm in a position that someone wants to give me advice. I follow my gut because in the end that's all you have. I shied away from playing just "the girl" roles because I didn't find them inspiring. I wanted to be taken seriously. I wanted to be challenged. I wanted to push myself to the limit. I wanted to; I want to do all that. That's where my passion lies, and it's not just playing the arm candy.[45]

By keeping her promise to herself in spite of the odds, Hilary Swank was about to embark on some of the most challenging projects of her life.

Chapter 5

A Force to Be Reckoned With

Hilary Swank proved her talent with her breakthrough performance in *Boys Don't Cry*, but her follow-up roles did not always afford her the same attention from audiences and critics. She stayed true to her personal code of being involved only in projects that intrigued and challenged her, but for various reasons they failed to live up to their potential. It did not stop her from continuing the search for worthy roles and learning how to improve herself professionally and personally. Her persistence would again pay off as it had earlier in her career so that by the end of 2004, Swank would prove once and for all that she was one of the most powerful film stars of her generation

Swank's search for challenging projects also extended to her personal life in New York City. One of the most time-consuming objectives she undertook was decorating the Greenwich Village townhouse she and her husband purchased in 2002 for almost $4 million. Due to their busy schedules, the spacious, two-story dwelling was not one that the couple spent a lot of time in when it was first purchased. In time, they began looking for ways to decorate it and considered it a work in progress. According to Swank: "Chad and I never see something as a done deal. We're a work in progress. It's a work in progress."[46]

When not personally involved with picking out furniture or antiques for her new home, Hilary Swank was considering a number of new projects. She had just a few weeks' respite to return to Greenwich Village when in June 2002 she decided on her next project, which would begin production in the fall. She had agreed to begin work on one of the most ambitious projects of her career.

Iron-Jawed Angels

The project was called *Iron-Jawed Angels*, and it recounts some of the almost forgotten events that earned American women the right to vote. "I wanted to call all my girlfriends after I read the script," said Swank. "I was really moved by the drive and courage of these women."[47] The filmmakers had a mammoth task in trying to compress the decades-long struggle into just a few hours in a way that would be meaningful to a contemporary audience. The cable network

Hilary Swank speaks with costar Julia Ormond at the post-premiere party for Iron-Jawed Angels. *The HBO film received high praise from critics.*

HBO helped finance the project and planned to air it when it was completed.

A Difficult Role

Swank played Alice Paul, another real-life character of single-minded determination. It was another challenge for the actress who, with extensive research, found a way to connect to the character. "I had a hard time trying to figure out a way to play her," Swank said. "She was a perfectionist, very much like me. She was a strong woman, very much like me. . . . But she was not sympathetic, and I had to reach down very far to let myself play her as she was, not as I might dream she was. . . . I realized that beneath it all, she was an outsider. And if there's one thing I relate to, it's that."[48]

The screenplay had several writers, including Sally Robinson, who also painstakingly researched the events to be re-created.

Alice Paul broadcasts news about the National Women's Party in this 1922 photo. Swank portrayed Paul in Iron-Jawed Angels.

The Real Alice Paul (1885–1977)

The success of *Iron-Jawed Angels* has prompted greater interest in the pioneering work of Alice Paul. The following is the recent entry on Biography.com.

Social reformer and lawyer, [Alice Paul was] born in Moorestown, New Jersey. Influenced by her Quaker family, she studied at Swarthmore (1905) and went on to do graduate work in New York City and England. While in London (1906–9) she worked in a settlement house, and was jailed on three occasions for suffragist actions. She took her Ph.D. from the University of Pennsylvania (1912), the same year she became chair of the congressional committee of the National American Suffrage Association. Impatient with its policies, in 1913 she helped to found the more militant Congressional Union for Woman Suffrage, which merged in 1917 to form the National Woman's Party, and she became chair (1942). After women won the right to vote with the 19th Amendment (1920), she devoted herself to gaining equal rights for women, and in 1923 introduced the first equal-rights amendment in Congress. She had meanwhile studied the law and broadened her field to the international arena, and although she did not live to see an equal rights amendment to the US Constitution, she did get an equal rights affirmation in the preamble to the United Nations charter.

Biography on A & E, "Paul, Alice." www.biography.com/search/article.jsp?aid=9435021.

The story begins with Alice Paul and her colleague Lucy Burns taking on the responsibilities of organizing a parade to promote woman suffrage. The parade turned into a riot, and Paul and Burns, who were more radical than many of the older members of the movement, decided to strike out on their own.

Support for woman suffrage grew, but in 1917, when the nation entered World War I, many sympathizers abandoned the cause, believing that it was unpatriotic to continue the fight when the country was at war. Alice Paul continued with her cohorts, however, and some of them were jailed on bogus charges. "What is astonishing to many people is they don't remember reading about this in their history books because it's not there," Robinson noted. "Imprisoning women unconstitutionally is a whole embarrassing sequence of events in American history." Robinson adds, "We just won't tell it."[49]

While in prison, Alice Paul began a hunger strike. As a result, she and the other suffragettes were force-fed through rubber hoses, their jaws forced open by metal clamps. Word got to the media, who dubbed the women "iron-jawed angels." Public outcry secured their release, popular support for woman suffrage regained strength, and in 1920 the Nineteenth Amendment to the Constitution granted women the right to vote.

Making *Angels*

Shot on location in Richmond, Virginia, *Iron-Jawed Angels* took four months to film, which was over a month longer than scheduled. Part of the delay was due to the nearby sniper shootings that made national headlines in the fall of 2002. For a month random shootings occurred in five states, leaving eleven out of thirteen victims dead. As a result of this event, the production briefly shut down and was continued again under heightened security until the two snipers were caught. Director Katja von Garnier and Hilary Swank organized the crew for a charity drive to help the victims of the attacks and their families.

While the film was in production, Swank again approached her role with the intensity for which she had become known. To lend reality to the extended prison sequence, she lost weight and even spent days wearing a blindfold to effectively approximate Alice Paul's sensitivity to light after being kept in solitary confinement.

The end result of the entire production was most impressive, and when the show premiered on the HBO cable network on February 2, 2004, critics reacted with overwhelming praise. Viewers were enthralled by the story that Swank's real-life character, Alice Paul, had called "a fight that shouldn't have even been a fight."[50]

On Location

After completing her work on *Iron-Jawed Angels* in December, Hilary Swank had some time to decide on her next project. She decided to star in an independent film that would be shot on location

Swank poses on the red carpet at the Toronto Film Festival, where her film Red Dust *won acclaim.*

Branching Out

In August 2002, Hilary Swank was in Los Angeles filming the independent feature *11:14* with an all-star ensemble cast. She was initially asked to play a larger role in the film but preferred a minor character instead. The script for the dark comedy-thriller written by Greg Marcks was so impressive that Swank also became one of seven executive producers on the project.

The main attraction of the independently made film was the narrative style of Marcks, who also debuted as a director on the project. The film opens with a fatal car accident that takes place at 11:14 P.M., and the story line then backtracks with a series of apparently unrelated stories. Swank's character is accused of something of which she is innocent, but like all the stories, her story connects to the accident that opens the film.

11:14 played several film festivals and was even nominated for best picture at France's Deauville Festival but was never seen in general release. In October 2005, it surfaced on DVD, and critics such as *San Francisco Chronicle*'s Mick LaSalle found it a worthwhile project. He added, "Swank plays Buzzy, a hapless store clerk, probably the only truly ingenuous character in the film."

Mick LaSalle, "Stars Pop Up in Clever, Dark, Little-Known Indie," *San Francisco Chronicle*, August 12, 2005, p. E-5.

in South Africa. Based on a popular book, *Red Dust* deals with the controversial issue of apartheid, the system in which the white minority governed the black majority. Swank agreed to play Sarah Barcant, a lawyer exiled to America but who returns to post-apartheid South Africa to participate in the nation's Truth and Reconciliation hearings.

Unfortunately, the film was unable to find an American distributor in spite of positive reactions at the Toronto and Seattle film festivals. It may yet find an appreciative audience if it manages to become available on DVD. On the plus side, Swank acquired yet another pet dog during the making of the film to add to her growing menagerie.

Hilary and Maggie

Red Dust aside, Hilary Swank was amassing an impressive body of work for audiences to appreciate. Her next project would leave little doubt in anyone's mind that Hilary Swank was one of the best actors of her generation. *Million Dollar Baby* is based on a series of short stories by F.X. Toole entitled *Rope Burns*. The screenplay by Paul Haggis centers on Maggie Fitzgerald, a thirty-two-year-old waitress from a Missouri trailer park whose only dream is to make it as a boxer in Los Angeles. She wants Frankie Dunn, a burned-out veteran of the boxing game who is totally against women in the ring, to train her. Dunn tells Fitzgerald that her gender aside, at thirty-two she is too old to begin training as a boxer. After much persistence by Fitzgerald, and with help from his only friend, a former boxer named Scrap Iron Dupres, Dunn trains Fitzgerald and becomes her surrogate father. The story then builds to an emotional and surprising conclusion.

It was the perfect marriage of actor to character, although Swank was not the first person offered the role. Producers had first approached both Sandra Bullock and Ashley Judd, but a scheduling conflict and financial considerations ruled them out. It was then that Hilary Swank was asked to consider the role. Swank read the script in one sitting and called the producers back immediately. She was told the next step was to meet Clint Eastwood, since he would be directing and costarring as Frankie Dunn along with Morgan Freeman as Scrap Iron.

An appointment was set up on the Warner Brothers lot for Swank to meet the cinema icon. On the drive to the studio, she passed the Oakwood Apartments she and her mother had lived in when they first arrived in Hollywood. "I got chills all over," she recalled. "When I drove up to the lot and said, 'I'm Hilary Swank, I'm here to meet Clint Eastwood,' all the while remembering how

I used to drive past that same spot praying that someday I'd get to work there, it was one of those moments when I was reminded how fortunate I am."[51]

Transforming the Body

Clint Eastwood suggested that Swank start working out to be physically in shape for the part, and Swank immediately undertook a grueling regimen. For the next three months, she trained like a professional boxer, changing her diet and sleep habits and doing intense physical workouts. The seemingly overwhelming preparation was just the kind of thing for which Swank was becoming known.

Her diet consisted of massive amounts of protein to allow her body to bulk up. She continually drank protein shakes as well as consuming raw fish and egg whites. She set the alarm to wake herself up in the middle of the night to consume more protein. Her body weight went from 110 pounds (50 k) to 129 pounds (59 k), much of it muscle.

The superb script for **Million Dollar Baby** *and the prospect of working with actor and director Clint Eastwood (pictured) led Swank to pursue a role in the film.*

Hilary Swank's workout schedule consisted of five hours a day with Eastwood's personal trainer in California, and later with well-known boxing trainer Hector Roca at New York's famous Gleason's Gym, which continued as filming went into production. Although she had been physically active all her life, the transformation into Maggie Fitzgerald was a landmark experience. "I can genuinely say I went through the most amazing experience of my life as far as my body is concerned," said Swank. "I felt so full of strength and power. Women are so used to feeling vulnerable, but I felt I could walk down any street at any time of the night and no one could harm me."[52]

Being Maggie

Another aspect of Swank's training was learning to think like a boxer. It proved difficult at first as she constantly apologized every time she hit her opponent during training. She quickly changed her thinking as her training progressed. She also learned how it felt to be hit as well as the mind-set required to hit somebody else.

By the time filming began, Hilary Swank not only looked like a boxer but thought, acted, and, most importantly, moved like a boxer. The transformation was complete, but to maintain her well-honed appearance, the training continued well after filming began. "Hilary doesn't study a character as much as burrows into it," said screenwriter Paul Haggis. "She doesn't decide how a character walks, she just nudges the girl forward, and the newly formed tissue determines her gait."[53]

As Hilary Swank maintained her training during production, the constant wear and tear on her body resulted in a life-threatening situation. On one occasion she popped a blister that appeared on top of another blister, and a staph infection developed. She was rushed to the hospital, where a doctor told her that such an infection, left untreated for another hour or two, would have killed her. "I didn't tell Clint, because in the end, that's what happens to boxers," said Swank. "They get blisters, they get infected. They have injuries and they keep pushing through it."[54]

Triumph and Controversy

Million Dollar Baby was completed on time and on budget, as was often the case with Clint Eastwood's films. Warner Brothers was so pleased with the result they chose to release it for a limited Los Angeles run in December 2004 in order to qualify for that year's Oscars, to be awarded in February 2005. Their strategy paid off, since most critics in the country were calling it a top contender for best film of the year.

Singled out for unanimous praise was Hilary Swank's performance. Audiences and critics alike were moved by Swank's subtle yet powerful portrayal of the trailer park native who dreamed of becoming a boxer. As she had in the past, Hilary Swank connected with her character in an uncommon way and went even further in translating that to the audience.

Not everyone who saw the film, however, approved of one important aspect of the plot. The dramatic turn the story takes in the last quarter stirred controversy among some viewers. Film critic Michael Medved gave away the ending to his readers, saying he had a moral obligation to do so. Conservative radio commentator Rush Limbaugh angrily took Eastwood to task on his show for the film's controversial ending. When Hilary Swank was asked about it during interviews, her point of view was diplomatic yet straightforward. "I don't think you have to agree when you're playing a person in a movie, and do everything they would do," she said. "You're acting. That was integral to the story, so I did it."[55]

Back on Top

When the award season began in 2005, Hilary Swank's name was consistently mentioned among the main contenders for recognition. She won the Golden Globe for best actress, a Screen Actors Guild Award, and several others. She was again Oscar nominated for her performance, and when the show was broadcast in February 2005, her name was announced as best actress of the year. Among the other awards handed out, Morgan Freeman was named best supporting actor, Clint Eastwood was named best director, and *Million Dollar Baby* was named best picture.

For her convincing portrayal of a boxer in **Million Dollar Baby** *(left), Swank receives the best actress Academy Award (below).*

Although only thirty years old, Hilary Swank had become one of the most honored actors of her time, earning two Academy Awards for her impressive performances. She would credit a large degree of luck for her prestigious position in the competitive industry, but luck played its part in tandem with preparation of extraordinary thoroughness. In a relatively short time, Swank's perseverance, single-mindedness, and unswerving dedication to her craft earned her accolades she humbly accepted. Having worked excessively hard to reach her position of respectability, she now had all the tools at her command to maintain a career of impressive skill and artistry.

Chapter 6

From This Moment On

Hilary Swank was now in the rare position of being able to take her career anywhere she wanted. Having established herself as one of the best actors of her time, she was free to choose any project she wanted that would express ideas and concepts that were important to her. What she chose were projects that continued to challenge both her own and her audience's expectations of her as she continued to grow as an actor and as a human being.

Accomplice Productions

In order to find and develop projects, she and her husband formed their own production company entitled Accomplice Productions. "We like the idea of being accomplices to talent,"[56] she explained.

Their first joint venture with this new production company was a break from the more serious endeavors Hilary Swank had pursued. As a change of pace that proved just as challenging, Swank and Lowe produced a game show with a relaxed premise based on their favorite parlor game, charades. With the popularity of such shows as *Celebrity Poker*, Swank and Lowe decided to produce a show in which several of their celebrity friends would join them for dinner and then play charades for money, with the proceeds going to charity. The cable channel American Movie

Classics liked the idea and aired five days of half-hour episodes in June 2005.

Besides the game show, Hilary Swank was also considering her next acting role. Now in her thirties, she no longer was interested in playing young girls who are just realizing their dreams or figuring out what they want from life. "I get scripts now, great scripts sometimes, that I'm just too emotionally mature for,"[57] she said.

The Black Dahlia

As she had done throughout her professional life, Hilary Swank again chose something that would be a creative challenge for her and a surprise for her legion of fans. The project was *The Black Dahlia*, a fictionalized version of one of the most bizarre unsolved murder mysteries in American history.

Based on the best-selling novel of the same name by popular novelist James Ellroy, *The Black Dahlia* concerns the strange death of Elizabeth Short, a struggling young actor. Los Angeles police uncovered her dismembered remains in 1947, and the case was given its name due to a small tattoo of the flower found on her torso. The investigative trail led to some important people in Los Angeles and Hollywood, but the case remains unsolved to this day.

Swank and her husband share a close moment. The couple formed their own production company in 2005.

Ellroy often writes about actual crimes, but filmmakers shy away from trying to do justice to the complicated story lines and characters of his popular books. A rare exception was the 1997 film version of Ellroy's novel *L.A. Confidential*, which also incorporated fictional and real-life elements of vintage Hollywood. Developing a script for *The Black Dahlia* turned out to be so difficult that the original screenwriter-director had to be replaced. Director Brian De Palma, known for such controversial films as *Dressed to Kill* (1980) and *Scarface* (1983), agreed to take over the project.

De Palma went about casting his film with some of the best young actors in Hollywood, including Josh Hartnett and Aaron Eckhart as the fictional detectives investigating the case. Swank was approached about taking on the role of a sexy woman who bears a striking resemblance to the victim. According to De Palma, "I've known Hilary for many years and I've always wanted her to play the sexy woman that she is. And she's never done it, so she took it as a great opportunity to do that."[58]

Madeline Sprague

Just prior to shooting the film, the project was embroiled in controversy. Fox News reported that De Palma was planning to use a thirteen-year-old girl in a sex scene, but quickly recanted the story when it was proved to be unfounded. That issue faded away, but another arose when financing for the project fell through. It took some time to get backing for the 40-million-dollar budget, but eventually, international financing was arranged in order for filming to begin. The movie was filmed partly in Los Angeles but mostly in Sofia, Bulgaria, since Hollywood bore little resemblance to the way it looked in 1947. Other difficulties during and after production delayed the opening of the highly anticipated film, which did not appear in theaters until 2006. Hilary Swank was cast as Madeline Sprague, a character described in the novel as "a knockout in a skirt and a tight cashmere sweater."[59]

Sprague becomes romantically involved with one of the detectives, and her family is also connected with the mystery surround-

The Black Dahlia gave Swank a chance to play a glamorous role. She is pictured here in a scene with Josh Hartnett.

ing the grisly murder. The appeal of the role was in doing something different. "I play the femme fatale which is nothing I've done before, and that's going to be fun—really beautiful costumes, really fun makeup," said Swank. "You know women really did it up back then! You couldn't leave the house without your hair done proper. I can't really imagine living like that."[60]

From True Crime to the Supernatural

In March 2005, while completing her scenes in *The Black Dahlia*, Swank finalized the agreement for her next project. It was one that allowed her to continue challenging herself and audiences' expectations of her. Entitled *The Reaping*, the film is a horror-thriller that producers had been looking to film since 2002.

Swank plays a university professor who prides herself on her ability to debunk myths and miracles scientifically. She is approached by a stranger who tells her of a town in Texas in which the ten plagues of the Bible are about to occur. Written by several different screenwriters, including brothers Cary Hayes and

9/11 Documentary

Prior to beginning work on *The Reaping*, Hilary Swank agreed to lend her talent to a project that was very close to her heart. She and actor Kevin Costner were approached individually by producers to narrate *On Native Soil: The Documentary of the 9/11 Commission Report*, which details the terrorist attacks on America in 2001. Swank had helped in the rescue effort following the attack in New York and also set up a shelter for displaced animals. She and Costner both readily agreed to the project. "I was in lower Manhattan that horrible day," Swank said. "I was drawn to the project by the amazing stories of the 9/11 families and survivors featured in the film, and I am proud that by contributing my voice to the project, I can help their voices to be heard."

Quoted in IMDb, "Swank and Costner to Narrate 9/11 Film," July 20, 2005. www.imdb.com/name/nm0005476/news.

Chad Hayes, the story takes some strange twists along the way. Chad Hayes said, "She's always been able to prove scientifically there are no miracles, and [we] tell you why, and then she comes across something she can't [disprove]. But it's a scary journey, really scary, to get her there."[61]

Katrina's Wrath

Just as production was about to begin on *The Reaping*, the long-delayed project underwent major changes. The original director left the project, and the locale was switched from Texas to Baton Rouge, Louisiana. The director's reasons for leaving were undisclosed, but it is known that Louisiana had offered the production tax incentives that saved money on the film's overall budget.

With a cast, crew, and location finally decided upon, Hilary Swank's reputation of dedication and talent preceded her into the production. "This is exciting for us," producer Joel Silver said. "She is fantastic, and it's a great opportunity to do something special with a really great actress."[62]

Ironically, production of the horror film detailing biblical destruction was forced to shut down when Hurricane Katrina struck the Gulf Coast in August 2005, leaving devastation in its wake. Louisiana was hit the hardest, and massive flooding added to the disaster when levees in New Orleans were breached.

It was at first thought that the production of The Reaping would be permanently halted due to the devastation. However, director Stephen Hopkins publicly addressed the issue in September: "On behalf of our cast and crew, we are pleased to be able to complete our filming in Louisiana and to be part of the region's recovery effort."[63]

Hurricane Katrina devastated parts of Baton Rouge, Louisiana (pictured), forcing the suspension of filming of The Reaping.

Pictured in happier times, Swank and her husband stunned fans in 2006 when they disclosed plans to divorce.

On the Home Front

The remainder of *The Reaping*'s production was completed without incident, leaving Swank available for other projects. The next endeavor to occupy her time was not a professional one but concerned her personal life. She and her husband made another major purchase that fueled speculation concerning their home life.

Hilary Swank and Chad Lowe bought a family-sized mansion in her hometown of Bellingham, Washington, in September 2005. Although they still maintained their Greenwich Village townhouse, the five-bedroom Bellingham house cost the couple $3.5 million.

The speculation that grew out of the purchase concerned whether or not they were planning on finally starting a family. The couple had been fielding questions concerning just that issue whenever they were interviewed. "Chad wants babies," Swank said. "I do, too, but not quite yet. . . . For Chad, he's there already. Any time I say to him, 'Hey, guess what?,' he looks at me and says, 'You want a baby?' I wouldn't describe it as an issue—well, maybe, it's definitely out there—but it will happen."[64]

A few months after purchasing the house in Bellingham, Hilary Swank and Chad Lowe publicly announced their separation in January 2006. Remaining devoted to their privacy, the couple would not publicly comment on the reasons, but the trial separation became official following the holiday season.

Swank's fans were disheartened by the news, but the talented Oscar winner remained hopeful. Swank and Lowe have both agreed to counseling to help reconcile their differences and maintain their relationship. "It's not over, we're not divorced," said Swank. "We've been together for over 13 years and there's a lot of love there. . . . We're still married."[65] Later in 2006, the couple —who remain friends—announced plans to divorce.

Freedom Writers

Hilary Swank dealt with the separation by focusing her considerable energy on her next project. It turned out to be one in which she would also serve as executive producer, an indication of her commitment to the story. As with Teena Brandon and Maggie Fitzgerald, Swank would play a character who had a dream and the determination to see it through. Only this time the dream was to help others.

Freedom Writers is based on a book written by Erin Gruwell and her students at Woodrow Wilson High School in Long Beach, California. In the fall of 1994, Gruwell was fresh out of college and preparing to face the students of room 203 in Wilson High. These young people—African American, Hispanic, Asian, and Caucasian—had grown up mostly in the roughest neighborhoods of Long Beach, rife with drugs, gangs, and violence. They had long felt abandoned by the education system and actually made bets on when Ms. Gruwell would quit the class.

It was rough going for the novice teacher, but she discovered something by accident that she ingeniously used to help motivate her students. When she intercepted a racially motivated caricature

The film Freedom Writers *is based on a book about gangs and violence in Long Beach, California.*

that was being passed around the room, she angrily told her students that such thinking was not unlike what the Nazis did to the Jews during World War II. When Gruwell asked the class if they were familiar with the Holocaust, no one raised a hand. She then asked if anyone in the room had ever been shot at, and every student raised a hand.

She then had her class read several books, most notably Anne Frank's *Diary of a Young Girl*, which slowly motivated them to begin discussing their own troubled lives in comparison to that of the young Holocaust victim. Gruwell then had the students begin their own diaries, encouraging the students to write honestly. Their anonymity was also ensured so they would not be judged harshly by their peers or other acquaintances who may read their entries. They dubbed themselves the Freedom Writers in honor of the Freedom Riders of the 1960s Civil Rights Movement. "Writing about the adversities we faced was definitely upsetting, but it was also a cathartic process that none of us would give back," wrote one student. "We were able to finally validate our pain, share it with our peers, and realize that we were not alone in our struggles."[66]

All of the 150 Freedom Writers graduated from high school, many went on to college, and some even became teachers in the district. *The Freedom Writers Diary* was published and became a national best seller, which resulted in Gruwell and her students making many public appearances on behalf of their project to encourage others to realize their dreams.

The inspiring story of Gruwell and her students was definitely in keeping with the kind of projects Hilary Swank wanted to be involved in. Production of *The Freedom Writers* with Swank as Erin Gruwell began in November 2005. Many of the original students can be seen as extras in the film.

Other Possibilities

After *The Freedom Writers*, Swank again wanted to change gears and challenge herself creatively by doing comedy, as she had done when she started in TV. "The crazy thing is that my mom thinks the biggest joke of all is that I won an Academy Award for best dramatic actress," Swank said. "She thinks that it's well deserved, but my mom knows me as this silly, like crazy, funny person. I started my career in comedy."[67] She has not yet found such a project but is still looking.

Another possibility would be a return to the stage, for the fiasco associated with the revival of *The Miracle Worker* did not deter her ambition to work in live theater again. Another revival was considered when she was offered the female lead in Arthur Miller's *After the Fall*, a fictionalized account of the playwright's relationship with his then wife, film icon Marilyn Monroe. Swank seriously considered the play until the script for *Million Dollar Baby* arrived on her doorstep.

Other actors have successfully juggled stage and film projects, and Hilary Swank will more than likely do the same, since it is a major priority for her. "I want to make sure that I'm doing theater too because that's what's inspiring to me," she said. "Unfortunately it seems like I'm doing a movie every time that the play comes along that I think I could be a part of, but I believe in fate—I really think it'll work out. I really love LOVE theater. It's a totally different feeling; it's just so different."[68]

Whatever she chooses to do next will certainly be a challenge to herself as well as her audience, since that is what she has preferred throughout her career. It may not have seemed likely that

Hilary Swank—who has proved her talent beyond all doubt—continues to boldly challenge herself and to surprise her audiences.

the shy, dreamy-eyed girl from the trailer park would succeed in seeing her dreams come true, but Hilary Swank has always risen to a challenge. It is what keeps her going and fires her up creatively. This is not only reflected in her personal successes but in the characters and projects she has chosen.

As she tackles each new role, the experience also expands her personal horizon as a humanitarian. Her performance in *Boys Don't Cry* led to her getting involved in organizations that counsel young adults struggling with a sexual identity crisis. Living in New York during the terrorist attack of 9/11 inspired her to become deeply involved in the relief effort. When the sniper attacks occurred in the Richmond area during the making of *Iron-Jawed Angels*, she spearheaded efforts to help the victims' families. The devastation of Hurricane Katrina during the filming of *The Reaping* motivated her to participate in the celebrity charity events that raised money for the victims of the storm.

She is also the first to admit that in spite of winning two Academy Awards by the age of thirty, she is still a work in progress. "I still have a lot to learn and I'm excited about that," she said. "I like watching performances and learning from them. God forbid if I ever watch anything I do and go 'Oh yeah, that was great. I couldn't change anything.' Then I might as well quit because where do you go?"[69]

From her trailer park in Bellingham to the stage of the Academy Awards, Hilary Swank has proven that nothing is impossible. As she continues to mature as a dedicated talent and as a human being, audiences will continue to be enthralled, inspired, and encouraged by her ability to transform her dreams into reality.

Chapter 1: Trailer Park Dreams

1. Quoted in Michelle Tauber, "Heroine Chic," *People*, April 14, 2003, p. 84.
2. Quoted in Tauber, "Heroine Chic," p. 83.
3. Quoted in Ingrid Sischy, "Hilary Swank in the Ring with the Movies' Fighting Spirit," *Interview*, March 2005, p. 186.
4. Hilary Swank, "Hilary Swank's Aha! Moment," Oprah.com. www.oprah.com/rys/omag/rys_omag_200109_swank.jhtml.
5. Quoted in Lorraine Ali, "Girls Don't Cry," *Newsweek*, January 10, 2005, p. 32.
6. Quoted in Carl Fussman, "Women We Love: Hilary Swank," *Esquire*, August 2002, p. 73.
7. Quoted in Lori Berger, "Hilary Swank—'I Never Expect Anything—That Way I Won't Be Disappointed,'" *Redbook*, March 2005, p. 89.
8. Quoted in Sischy, "Hilary Swank in the Ring with the Movies' Fighting Spirit," p. 184.
9. Quoted in CBS News, "Hilary Swank: Oscar Gold," *60 Minutes* transcript, March 2, 2005. CBS.com/stories/2005/03/02/60II/main677647.shtml.
10. Quoted in Sischy, "Hilary Swank in the Ring with the Movies' Fighting Spirit," p. 184.

Chapter 2: The Art of Persistence

11. Quoted in Sischy, "Hilary Swank in the Ring with the Movies' Fighting Spirit," p. 184.
12. Quoted in *Million Dollar Baby*, DVD, directed by Clint Eastwood. Burbank, CA: Warner Home Video, 2005.
13. Quoted in Sischy, "Hilary Swank in the Ring with the Movies' Fighting Spirit," p. 186.
14. Quoted in Berger, "Hilary Swank—'I Never Expect Anything—That Way I Won't Be Disappointed,'" p. 89.
15. Quoted in *Buffy the Vampire Slayer*, DVD, directed by Fran

Rubel Kuzui. New York: 20th Century Fox Home Entertainment, 2001.

16. Quoted in James Kaplan, "That Girl," *Premiere*, September 2001, p. 71.
17. Quoted in Fussman, "Women We Love," p. 73.
18. Quoted in *People*, "50 Most Beautiful People," May 8, 2000, p. 192.
19. Quoted in Scott Brown, "And in This Corner," *Entertainment Weekly*, December 24, 2004, p. 36.
20. Quoted in Berger, "Hilary Swank—'I Never Expect Anything—That Way I Won't Be Disappointed,'" pp. 90–91.
21. Quoted in Johanna Schneller, "A Woman in Full," *In Style*, August 2001, p. 244.
22. Quoted in Louis B. Hobson, "The Sleeping Beauty," Canoe—Jam! May 5, 2002. http://jam.canoe.ca/Movies/Artists/S/Swank_Hilary/2002/05/22/762107.html.
23. Quoted in Berger, "Hilary Swank—'I Never Expect Anything—That Way I Won't Be Disappointed,'" p. 90.

Chapter 3: Dreams Do Come True

24. Quoted in J. Oliver Nixon, "Isn't She Swank," *Gotham*, May 2002, p. 86.
25. Quoted in Ruthe Stein, "Hilary Swank Playing Oscars by Ear," *San Francisco Chronicle*, March 19, 2000, p. 33.
26. Quoted in Edward Helmore, "Based on a True Story," *Dazed and Confused*, April 2000, p. 67.
27. Quoted in Cynthia Amsden, "Hilary Swank: The *Boys Don't Cry* Star Tells Us What It Takes to Be a Man," *Tribute*, March 2000, p. 38.
28. Quoted in Dave Karger, "Boy on the Side," *Entertainment Weekly*, October 29, 1999, p. 24.
29. Quoted in Karger, "Boy on the Side," p. 25.
30. Quoted in Fussman, "Women We Love," p. 73.
31. Quoted in Michael Giltz, "Hilary's Journey," *Advocate*, March 28, 2000, p 35.
32. Quoted in CBS News, "Hilary Swank."

Chapter 4: The Challenge of Success

33. Quoted in Hillary deVries, "Seriously Swank," *W*, December 2000, p. 365.
34. Quoted in *Time*, "She's a Big Girl Now," January 17, 2000, p. 88.
35. Quoted in Stein, "Hilary Swank Playing Oscars by Ear," p. 33.
36. Quoted in *The Affair of the Necklace*, DVD, directed by Charles Shyer. Burbank, CA: Warner Home Video, 2002.
37. Quoted in Kaplan, "That Girl," p. 70.
38. Quoted in Donna Freydkin, "Back in the Ring," *USA Today*, January 28, 2005, p. 01D.
39. Quoted in Nixon, "Isn't She Swank," pp. 84–85.
40. Quoted in Louis B. Hobson, "Insomnia Lured A-list Actors," Canoe—Jam! May 25, 2002. http://jam.canoe.ca/Movies/Artists/N/Nolan_Christopher/2002/05/25/760567.html.
41. Quoted in *Insomnia*, DVD, directed by Christopher Nolan. Burbank, CA: Warner Home Video, 2002.
42. Quoted in *Insomnia*.
43. Quoted in Hobson, "The Sleeping Beauty."
44. Quoted in Martha Frankel, "Hilary Swank: Beating the Odds," *Biography*, March 2003, p. 47.
45. Quoted in Christy Lemire, "Hilary Swank: Flexing Her Acting Muscles Five Years After Her Oscar Turn in 'Boys Don't Cry,' the Former Bellingham Resident Is Back in Another Demanding and Lauded Role, as a Boxer in 'Million Dollar Baby,'" *Seattle Times*, January 6, 2005, p. C1.

Chapter 5: A Force to Be Reckoned With

46. Quoted in Raul A. Barrenech, "At Home with Hilary Swank and Chad Lowe," *New York Times*, April 7, 2005, p. F1.
47. Quoted in *Iron Jawed Angels*, "Chat with Angels," video clip.http://iron_jawed-angels.com/multimedia.htm.
48. Quoted in Frankel, "Hilary Swank," p. 47.
49. Quoted in *Iron-Jawed Angels*, DVD, directed by Katja von Garnier, New York: HBO Home Video, 2004.
50. Quoted in *Iron-Jawed Angels*.
51. Quoted in Sischy, "Hilary Swank in the Ring with the Movies' Fighting Spirit," p. 186.

52. Quoted in Louise Gannon, "Sexy Lady," *Elle* (UK), April, 2005, pp. 122–23.
53. Paul Haggis, "Hilary Swank: Inhabitant of Imagined Lives," *Time*, April 18, 2005, p. 116.
54. Quoted in CBS News, "Hilary Swank."
55. Quoted in Brad Balfour, "Hilary Swank Hitting a Million," Pop Entertainment.com. www.popentertainment.com/swank.htm.

Chapter 6: From This Moment On

56. Quoted in Alexandra Jacobs, "Hilary Goes Wild!" *Allure*, July 2005, p. 144.
57. Quoted in Amy Bloom, "Portrait of an Artist: Hilary Swank Readies for the Next Fight," *Vitals*, March 2005, p. 131.
58. Quoted in Romain Desbiens, "Interview with Brian De Palma," Brian De Palma, May 23, 2005. http://briandepalma.online.fr/interviewdahlia.htm.
59. James Ellroy, *The Black Dahlia*. New York: Mysterious Press, 1988, p. 141.
60. Quoted in Jacobs, "Hilary Goes Wild!" p. 144.
61. Quoted in Sci Fi Wire, "Swank's *Reaping* Looks at Faith," April 25, 2005. www.scifi.com/scifiwire2005/index.php?category=3&id=30890.
62. Quoted in Killer Movies, "Hilary Swank to Star in Horror 'The Reaping,'" March 11, 2005. www.killermovies.com/r/thereaping/articles/5003.html.
63. Quoted in ComingSoon.net, "*The Reaping* Resumes Production," September 21, 2005. www.comingsoon.net/news/topnews.php?id=11288.
64. Quoted in Gannon, "Sexy Lady," p. 125.
65. Quoted in IMDb, "Swank and Lowe Trying to Save Marriage," January 18, 2006. www.imdb.com/news/wenn/2006-01-18#celeb1.
66. Quoted in Erin Gruwell Education Project, "Frequently Asked Questions." www.gruwellproject.org/site/pp.asp?c=bnJEJJPxB&b=79002.
67. Quoted in Stephen Schaefer, "Punch-Drunk Lady: Hilary

Swank Looks to Score Another Knockout in 'Million Dollar Baby,'" *Boston Herald*, December 26, 2004, p. 51.

68. Quoted in Hilary Rowland, "Exclusive Interview with Two-Time Oscar Winner Hilary Swank," *Hilary Magazine.* www.hilary.com/celebrity/hilary-swank.html.

69. Quoted in Balfour, "Hilary Swank Hitting a Million."

1974

Hilary Ann Swank is born on July 30 in Lincoln, Nebraska.

1983

The Swank family moves to a trailer park in Bellingham, Washington, where nine-year-old Hilary makes her professional acting debut in a local production of *The Jungle Book*. She also excels in gymnastics and swimming in the Junior Olympics, ranking fifth in the state as all-around gymnast.

1990

After her parents' separation, Hilary and her mother, Judy Swank, move to Los Angeles, while her father and older brother remain in Washington.

1991

Hilary Swank makes her TV acting debut in the comedy series *Harry and the Hendersons*; also appears on *Evening Shade, Growing Pains,* and *Camp Wilder.*

1992

Makes her film debut with a small role in the film *Buffy the Vampire Slayer.*

1994

Portrays the title character in *The Next Karate Kid.*

1996

Appears in the feature films *Kounterfeit* and *Sometimes They Come Back . . . Again* and the TV movie *Terror in the Family.*

1997

Appears in the film *Quiet Days in Hollywood;* appears in several

TV movies; marries actor Chad Lowe on October 2, after meeting at an MTV–sponsored sporting event.

1998

Swank is fired from TV's *Beverly Hills 90210*.

1999

Portrays real-life hate crime victim Teena Brandon in the film *Boys Don't Cry* to rave reviews.

2000

Wins several film awards for *Boys Don't Cry* and goes on to win an Oscar for best actress; has a small role in the horror film *The Gift*.

2001

Stars in the film *The Affair of the Necklace*.

2002

Plays detective Ellie Burr in *Insomnia*; buys and moves into a Greenwich Village brownstone with her husband.

2003

Fulfills childhood dream of playing an astronaut by starring in the science-fiction film *The Core*; stars in and produces the crime thriller *11:14*; in March appears in a stage production revival of *The Miracle Worker* in North Carolina, but the play closes before making it to Broadway.

2004

Stars as suffragette Alice Paul in the HBO movie *Iron-Jawed Angels* in February; stars in an apartheid film shot in South Africa called *Red Dust*; stars as boxer Maggie Fitzgerald in *Million Dollar Baby*, costarring and directed by Clint Eastwood.

2005

Wins a second Oscar for *Million Dollar Baby*, which also wins best picture; coproduces a cable-TV game show with her husband called *Celebrity Charades;* purchases a multimillion-dollar house in hometown of Bellingham, Washington.

2006

Announces plans to divorce; stars in the films *Black Dahlia* and *The Reaping;* produces and stars in the film *Freedom Writers;* begins filming *P.S. I Love You.*

Books

The Freedom Writers and Erin Gruwell, *The Freedom Writers Diary: How a Teacher and 150 Teens Used Writing to Change Themselves and the World Around Them.* New York: Broadway Books, 1999. The story and diary entries from the Long Beach, California, Wilson High students of Erin Gruwell and the basis for the film *The Freedom Writers.*

Martha A. Hotstetter et al., *2000 Current Biography Yearbook.* New York: Wilson, 2000. This is a compilation of short sketches of important people of the year and the sources in which more information may be found. The essay on Swank is on pages 543 to 545.

Aphrodite Jones, *All She Wanted: The Teena Brandon Story.* New York: Pocket Books, 1996. This is the first published account of the Teena Brandon story and was used for the film *Boys Don't Cry;* however, the writing style tends toward the lurid and the sensational.

Periodicals

Lorraine Ali, "Girls Don't Cry," *Newsweek*, January 10, 2005.

Lori Berger, "Hilary Swank—'I Never Expect Anything—That Way I Won't Be Disappointed,'" *Redbook*, March 2005.

Claire Bickley, "Humble Hilary," *Toronto Sun*, November 28, 2001.

Amy Bloom, "Portrait of an Artist: Hilary Swank Readies for the Next Fight," *Vitals*, March 2005.

Scott Brown, "And in This Corner," *Entertainment Weekly*, December 24, 2004.

Mark Caro, "Hilary Swank Fights Her Way Back to the Top," *Chicago Tribune*, December 17, 2004.

Richard Deitsch, "Q+A Hilary Swank," *Sports Illustrated*, January 10, 2005.

Stacy D'Erasmo, "Boy Interrupted," *Out*, October 1999.

Hillary deVries, "Seriously Swank," *W*, December 2000.

Martha Frankel, "Hilary Swank: Beating the Odds," *Biography*, March 2003.

Carl Fussman, "Women We Love: Hilary Swank," *Esquire*, August 2002.

Michael Giltz, "Hilary's Journey," *Advocate*, March 28, 2000.

Paul Haggis, "Hilary Swank: Inhabitant of Imagined Lives," *Time*, April 18, 2005.

Alexandra Jacobs, "Hilary Goes Wild!" *Allure*, July 2005.

James Kaplan, "That Girl," *Premiere*, September 2001.

David LaChapelle, "10 For Our Time," *Interview*, October 2004.

J. Oliver Nixon, "Isn't She Swank," *Gotham*, May 2002.

Robin Rauzi, "Girly Boy," *Austin-American Statesman*, December 6, 1999.

Ingrid Sischy, "SWANK!" *Interview*, April 2000.

Hilary Swank, "Hilary Swank's Aha! Moment," *Oprah Magazine*, September 2001.

Internet Sources

Brad Balfour, "Hilary Swank Hitting a Million," Pop Entertainment.com. www.popentertainment.com/swank.htm.

Rob Blackwelder, "Swagger-less Swank," SPLICEDwire.com, November 19, 2001. www.splicedonline.com/01features/hswank.html.

CBS.com, "Hilary Swank: Oscar Gold," *60 Minutes* transcript, March 2, 2005. www.cbs.com/stories/2005/03/02/60II/main 6T1647.shtml

Louis B. Hobson, "Fate Gives Hilary Swank a Helping Hand," Canoe—Jam! April 16, 2000. www.jam.canoe.ca/Movies/Artists/S/Swank_Hilary/2000/04/16/pf-762110.html.

———, "The Sleeping Beauty," Canoe—Jam! May 5, 2002. www.jam.canoe.ca/Movies/Artists/S/Swank_Hilary/2002/05/22/762107.html.

Terence Pillay, "Exclusive Interview with Hilary Swank," Going

Places, February 11, 2004. www.goingplacessa.com/article_detail.asp?Article_ID=327&Article_Year=2004.

Hilary Rowland, "Exclusive Interview with Two-Time Oscar Winner Hilary Swank," *Hilary Magazine*. www.hilary.com/celebrity/hilary-swank.html.

Jim Slotek, "Swank Attitude," Canoe—Jam! March 29, 2003. www.jam.canoe.ca/Movies/Artists/S/Swank_Hilary/2003/03/29/762103.html.

Mike Szymanski, "Hilary Swank Dons Her First Corset in 'Affair of the Necklace,'" Zap2it.com, November 27, 2001. www.zap2it.com/movies/features/profiles/story/0,1259,—-9826,00.html.

Zap2it.com, "Hilary Swank Chastised as a Child," November 19, 2001. www.zap2it.com/movies/news/story/0,1259,—-9720,00. html.

Web Sites

Hilary Swank Fan (http:/hilaryswankfan.com). This site boasts that it is the oldest fan-based Swank Web site on the Internet. There are contests for fans of Swank trivia, video downloads from her films and TV appearances, interviews, countless magazine clippings, and links to other fan sites.

Internet Movie Database (www.imdb.com). Includes a biography of Swank as well as pictures, external Web site links, details of her films, and daily updates of her projects.

Wondrous Hilary Swank (www.hswank.com). Here is another fan site dedicated to Swank. This easy-to-navigate site is updated almost weekly with Swank's various projects and current events.

DVDs

The Affair of the Necklace. Directed by Charles Shyer. Burbank, CA: Warner Home Video, 2002.

Boys Don't Cry. Directed by Kimberly Peirce. New York: 20th Century Fox Home Entertainment, 2000.

Iron-Jawed Angels. Directed by Katja von Garnier. New York: HBO Home Video, 2004.

Million Dollar Baby. Directed by Clint Eastwood. Burbank, CA: Warner Home Video, 2005.

Cover photo: Jim Ruymen/UPI/Landov
© Academy of Motion Picture Arts and Sciences/HO/epa/CORBIS, 72
Evan Agostini/Getty Images Entertainment/Getty Images, 53
© Bernard Annebicque/Sygma/CORBIS, 19
AP/Wide world Photos, 37, 44
© Bettmann/CORBIS, 66
© Hubert Boesl/dpa/CORBIS, 62
Vince Bucci/Getty Images Entertainment/Getty Images, 31
Gerard Burkhart/AFP/Getty Images, 28
Murray Close/Alcon Entertainment/The Kobal Collection, 55
Columbia Pictures/Photofest, 27
Hulton Archive/Getty Images, 48
© Karen Huntt/CORBIS, 13
© Mikael Karlsson/Alamy, 84
Rolf Konow/Universal/The Kobal Collection, 79
Peter Kramer/Getty Images Entertainment/Getty Images, 65
© Vincent Laforet/POOL/epa/CORBIS, 81
Arnaldo Magnani/ Getty Images Entertainment/Getty Images, 86
Mark Mainz/Getty Images Entertainment/Getty Images, 77, 82
Luis Martinez/Getty Images Entertainment/Getty Images, 47
© Mary Evans Picture Library/Alamy, 14
Bill Matlock, Fox Searchlight/The Kobal Collection, 43
Rob McEwan/Alcon Entertainment/Section Eight LTD/The Kobal Collection,
   58
Melissa Moseley/Alphaville/Lakeshore/The Kobal Collection, 51
© Lisa O'Connor/Zuma/CORBIS, 10
© Gregory Pace/CORBIS, 39
Paramount/Photofest, 61
Réunion des Musées Nationaux/Art Resource, NY, 54
© John Sturrock/Alamy, 23
© Sygma/CORBIS, 7
© Andrew Wallace/Reuters/CORBIS, 69
Merie W. Wallace/Warner Bros./The Kobal Collection, 75 (left)
Warner Bros. TV/The Kobal Collection, 25
Kevin Winter/Getty Images Entertainment/Getty Images, 75 (right)
Firooz Zahedi/Spelling/The Kobal Collection, 34e

Dwayne Epstein was born in Brooklyn, New York, and grew up in Southern California. His first professional writing credit was in 1982, writing newspaper film reviews and year-end analyses of popular culture.

Nationally, he has been a regular contributor to several film magazines since 1996. Internationally, he contributed to Bill Krohn's film book *Serious Pleasures* in 1997, which saw publication in Europe. Mr. Epstein has had several children's books published since 2000 and is currently writing a biography on actor Lee Marvin. Mr. Epstein also authored *People in the News: Adam Sandler, People in the News: Will Ferrell*, as well as *History Makers: Lawmen of the Old West*, all for Lucent Books. He lives in Long Beach, California, with his girlfriend, Barbara, and too many books on movie history.